Questions

from a

Life Watcher

Insights on Cultivating Inner Wisdom

Mary-Beth Klastorin, MSW, LCSW

BALBOA.
PRESS
A DIVISION OF HAY HOUSE

Balboa Press books may be ordered through booksellers or by contacting:

Balboa Press
A Division of Hay House
1663 Liberty Drive
Bloomington, IN 47403
www.balboapress.com
1 (877) 407-4847

Print information available on the last page.

ISBN: 978-1-5043-8459-9 (sc)
ISBN: 978-1-5043-8460-5 (e)

Balboa Press rev. date: 12/15/2017

This book is dedicated to those
courageous souls, brave enough to shine
light on the shadow side of self.

Contents

Acknowledgements

I KNOW THAT NOTHING GETS born into conception by itself. This process requires the help of others to breathe life into any creation. I ask the question, "How do I adequately thank those who helped to provide the spiritual nourishment to document my journey?" My inner voice says to simply say "thank you." So with grace and gratitude, I would like to acknowledge those who were instrumental in helping me grow as a person and as a soul.

First, I would like to thank my husband, Howard Elliot Eckstein, for his unconditional love, encouragement, editing support, and the space I needed for self-reflection. Without his love, this book would not have been born.

I wish to thank my editor and beloved friend, Pamela Accetta Smith, for her professional input and belief in my quest to find meaning.

My deceased parents, Milton and Janet, I thank for my life and their best efforts to love and nurture me. I want to particularly acknowledge my son for giving me the impetus to dig deeper, from flesh to heart. Thanks also to my two sisters and nieces, all of whom are mirrors that helped me to understand my roots and witness how energies from previous generations still live and thrive.

To my friends (you know who you are) I extend deep gratitude for seeing my goodness.

And lastly, my appreciation and thanks go to those teachers who held space for spiritual contemplation which became the impetus for self-examination and awareness. A special thank-you to Lawrence Phillips, my Feldenkrais® instructor, for the heart-felt space he held for me to practice the art of being a "Life-Watcher."

With deepest gratitude, I thank all those along the way who helped to remind me to "know thyself."

Foreword

"THE JOURNEY OF HEALING, like so many journeys, begins with humble, initiating steps. The healing of body and mind, heart and spirit is one of humanity's most noble endeavors and requires that we begin at the beginning, a process that is whole-heartedly embraced by *Questions from a Life Watcher*. The author, Mary-Beth Klastorin, LCSW, draws from a lifetime of clinical experience to provide pithy explorations into many of the themes involved with learning, healing and transforming. Accompanied by many of the great gems of humanity's wisdom, each chapter uses evocative quotations and probing questions to encourage a hands-on, heart-engaged exploration—a perfect primer and adjunct for psychotherapy, and is also elegantly functional for self-motivated students of the inner journey as well. Engaging our deeper selves on the path of healing is well served by drawing from this very useful and inspiring guide."

~ *Lawrence Phillips, for over thirty years a Guild Certified Feldenkrais Practitioner®*

An Invitation

THIS BOOK IS MY personal story about change, one that is universal, documenting my search to find meaning, purpose, and an understanding far greater than the small "self." I invite you, the reader, to join me as we explore a sense of one's inner life. Abraham Maslow, an American psychologist best known for his work, "Maslow's Hierarchy of Needs," said, "Human life will never be understood unless its highest aspirations are taken into account. The striving towards growth, self-actualization, health, the quest for identity and autonomy, the yearning for excellence are a widespread and perhaps a universal human tendency."

All these needs are identified by Dr. Maslow as important parts of human growth and development. However, without self-actualization and love, the evolution of the soul does not expand. We are spiritual beings in a physical body, born to be both student and teacher in search of our life's purpose. We learn about ourselves through our relationships as observers of both our stories and other people's stories. Maslow also said, "What is necessary to change a person is to change his/her awareness of self."

My deepest desire is to create a different story for my life. The late author, Merle Shain, wrote in *Hearts That We Broke*

Long Ago, "It takes many people a lifetime to begin to see the pattern to their lives and most never do. Which means that abandoned children remain abandoned, and victims cower on. And people who feel insecure as a child usually feel that way for some time more."

We, as social beings, evolve by our interactions with self and others. When we experience these exchanges, we develop beliefs from our life experiences that create our lives. The steps that help make changes are simple. Acknowledge that you have a story that you want to alter which, most often, is based on childhood events. Recognize those incidents that keep repeating themselves as old wounds needing to be acknowledged. Work on developing self-awareness by listening to your thoughts, experiencing your emotions, and focusing on your bodily sensations as they work in concert. This awakening is the beginning of changing your story.

Awareness can be developed by answering the questions at the end of each chapter of this book. View the table of contents to choose the questions that interest you or read the pages in sequential order. My queries are based on curiosity. There is often repetition in my questions. The reason being, that everything relates to everything else. This is illustrated by the Chinese philosophy of the five elements — earth, water, fire, wood and metal — which represents the interactions and relationships between all things.

Work with this book alone or share in a group setting. Your answers provide guidance for self-reflection and an avenue for the stories that need to be told — dulcet refrains that keep pointing back to your ability to learn what is most important for transformation. The process is like that of Dorothy in *The Wizard of Oz* being led down the path of the yellow brick road to understand that everything we need exists within.

Mary-Beth

What Does It Mean to
Nurture Myself?

N URTURING IS A SYNONYM for "caring for," and is the foundation of emotional health. The word "mother" is defined as a female that cares for a child's physical and emotional needs, and is associated with nurturing. It is through the daily interactions between mother and child that a bond is established. This interaction is the foundation for developing self-love and the ability to self-nurture. Anthony Biglan, author of *The Nurture Effect*, says, "Nearly all problems of human behavior stem from our failure to ensure that people live in environments that nurture their well-being."

I have my own story of not feeling nurtured or loved, one that has been woven into the text of this book. The very premise of self-love is the impetus to ask myself, "What does it mean to nurture myself?" My goal is to understand the missing piece that leaves a void in my life. Following this path of self-discovery led to an intergenerational tale of sorrow and suffering rooted in my female ancestors. They were not nurtured in the way that promoted their own growth and development. In turn, the ramifications were reflected in their parenting, as they were not able to nurture their children – and this created a lineage of pain.

So, I ask myself another question, "Do I nurture myself?" My response is, "Not well." Being aware of this gap in my development is important, but I realize it involves more. It is the attention to the details of nurturing that requires my action. The words "encouragement," "fostering," "coaching" and "recognizing" enter my thoughts. These are all verbs that entail active involvement in re-parenting self. This means changing my stories by developing and practicing a positive inner dialogue of words that cultivate self-love. I recognize the times when love is present and when it is not. I offer myself words of reassurance when I feel afraid. I become a cheerleader that rallies on my behalf when I need to believe in who I am. I am able to acknowledge when sadness and anger are present, and to respond by breathing or moving to feel like I am being cradled in my own arms.

Cultivating presence with what we see, touch, taste, smell and hear are also gifts of nourishment. I personally see colors and textures that visually promote love. I feel my heart beating and smell the sweet fragrances of flowers that lure me with their perfume. These sensory experiences instruct me to follow a stream of energy, and, like potpourri, they become a mixture that creates the belief in my own goodness. My being present with my own self-nurturing is an example of this being a possibility for all of us.

Questions to Explore:

1. Do you nurture yourself?

2. If so, in what ways do you self-nurture?

What Can a Tree Teach You?

A TREE IS A COMMON universal, archetypal symbol for mother, spiritual and intellectual development, plus death and rebirth. It is found in many traditions identified in ancient civilizations. Throughout the history of humankind, trees are referenced in mythology and religions such as Judaism, Christianity and Buddhism. They symbolize knowledge as it relates to life. For example, Buddha sat under the Bodhi Tree. Adam and Eve lived with the Tree of Life in paradise and ate from the tree of knowledge. The oak tree symbolizes strength. The branch of the olive tree represents peace. And we all have a family tree that traces our lineage that reflects our DNA as stories our ancestors pass on.

Trees have life-giving powers that heal and provide sustenance to the earth. They provide oxygen for the planet. Their branches reach out toward the sun, accepting nourishment, while their roots dig into the earth's soul, symbolically affirming spiritual growth.

It is astounding to watch a tree transform during its seasonal rotation. Their leaves fall in autumn, rejuvenate by sitting in dormancy during winter, reawaken with blossoms in spring, and bear fruit in summer. This cycle represents the cyclical nature of the seasons where growing, thriving, changing and transforming occur throughout the life span of each year. This same rotation found in nature is also a metaphor for human development that becomes enhanced when our physical and spiritual selves are unified.

Ian Shamir, writer and artist, gave his permission to quote his poem here, but requested that if I did so, that I tell his story about how he came to write this. He said, "It was one of those difficult days…one of those days that tore at the very roots of my being. I just had to get outside to breathe and somehow find a way back to my center, a return to the peace and clarity of my soul. I managed to open the front door with tears in my eyes. I began to move along the sidewalk, lifting one foot in front of the other without a clue where I was going. Exhausted, I leaned against a huge Cottonwood tree, the deep ridges of the bark held me close. I said, 'I've been working for you for many years now, planting thousands of trees, teaching about the miracles of the earth and now I need your help! Can you help me? I need some advice.' I felt the tree reach out to me, to wrap me in its branches, to comfort me as I leaned against its steady trunk. This old and wise Cottonwood tree spoke to me with clarity and wisdom. I felt hopeful, renewed, loved and went home and word-for-word wrote the following caring message from this tree friend."

"Advice from a Tree"®

Dear Friend
Stand Tall and Proud
Sink your roots deeply into the Earth
Reflect the light of your true nature
Think long term

Go out on a limb
Remember your place among all living things
Embrace with the joy of the changing seasons
For each yields its own abundance
The Energy and Birth of Spring
The Growth and Contentment of Summer
The Wisdom to let go of leaves in the Fall
The Rest and Quiet renewal of Winter
Feel the wind and sun
And delight in their presence
Look up at the moon that shines down upon you
And mystery of the stars at night
Seek nourishment from the good things in life
Simple pleasures
Earth, fresh air, light
Drink plenty of water
Be content with your natural beauty
Let your limbs sway and dance in the breezes
Be flexible
Remember your roots
Enjoy the view!

This poem is something that I treasure as a gift that provides the seeds for inner growth, all from a tree. I wear a silver necklace that I gave myself, a gift to represent the Tree of Life. This symbol reinforces my commitment to grow and evolve in my physical body and within my spirit. It also reminds me of the connection between the cycle of life found in nature, and that of humankind.

Questions to Explore:

1. What have you learned about your spiritual self from connecting with nature?

2. What are the connections to your roots that have helped you grow and evolve?

Are You Curious about Your Life?

WALT DISNEY WAS AN animator, cartoonist and voice actor who once said, "We keep moving forward, opening new doors, and doing new things, because we're curious and curiosity keeps leading us down new paths." When we are curious about something, we stay focused on what we want to understand.

I have been curious about my life and the stories that have allowed me to be an artist, sculpting and expanding new levels of awareness. As the poet and philosopher Ralph Waldo Emerson said, "Curiosity is lying in wait for every secret."

Uncovering the secrets from my family story has helped me develop compassion, enable forgiveness of self, and be far less judgmental towards others. This probably would not have occurred if I had not asked myself those pertinent questions about life. My drive to know opened me up to a life of possibilities and insights that created more questions and new levels of awareness.

Socrates is believed to have said, "The unexamined life is not worth living."

My own inquiries were continuous and began with one question, "Are you a Life Watcher?" This one query helped me become a life-explorer, courageous enough to journey across unknown territory. As I gained momentum, a rhythm and pace created a multitude of questions that helped me to dig, uncover, and investigate my inner self — the space where I hear my inner voice.

Humans are filled with curiosity. This makes becoming an explorer of our inner terrain an option available to all of us. When you begin with one question, more will appear. And like the breadcrumbs in the fairy tale of Hansel and Gretel, they will create a path to find your way home, back to your heart.

Questions to Explore:

1. What are some of the things that you are curious about?

2. What questions do you have about your inner life that is waiting to be revealed?

What Life Lessons Can You Learn?

O PRAH WINFREY'S MASTER CLASS seen on OWN
Television introduces the concept of using your life as a
class. Oprah says, "Everyone has a story and there is something
to be learned from every story." Our stories can help develop
introspection. For some, it may seem their life story is one of
accomplishment and connection. For others, it is repeated
suffering. It is as if a sorceress cast a spell for good or bad,
and the accumulation of what we see, hear and feel becomes
a paradigm for interpreting our environment. This type of
thinking becomes a habit that can evolve into the beliefs by
which one understands the world.

Tara Brach, in her book, *Awakening from the Trance of
Unworthiness*, talks about how crucial childhood experiences
are to one's life story. "Children need to feel like they belong and
to know that they are understood and loved," she says. These
initial relationships become the basis for our inner life, and when
a child's parents and close family members cannot provide this
space, the child often disconnects from his or her "self" and feels
alone. It is through a sense of belonging that emotional and social
development becomes the underpinning of the story of one's life.

When we become aware of what we are thinking and
feeling, our inner resources can be nurtured, thus planting

seeds for our heart center — the place in the body where love lives.

My outlook on life initially helped me navigate through personal obstacles. However, I grew to realize that the need for self-protection from rejection and failure became a barrier to feeling joy and peace. I pushed away pain by compulsively overeating or worrying about what "could" happen. In turn, these overbearing thoughts repeated a cycle of negativity.

It wasn't until I became mindful of my own life story that I discovered the antidote to my own spell — choosing a new direction for living in the world. This is when healing and transformation began. Oprah Winfrey's television show helped me to ask the question, "Can I use my own life story as a class?" When I answered "Yes," I began to recognize what I needed to learn, which in turn, fostered healing and transformation.

Questions to Explore:

1. How can you use your life story as a master class to learn, heal, and transform your life?

2. How might you use both the small and large milestone events of your life story to understand your inner self?

Do You Know Your Life's Purpose?

I FOUND A SECRET CODE that opened the door to my destiny. I didn't realize that this gift was lying dormant, just waiting to be discovered. With faith and hope as my confidantes, I felt encouraged to discover the secret that originated from my family DNA. This came in the form of an energetic pattern activated by my mother, grandmother, and great-grandmother, and carried over into all my relationships. Because of this pattern, I perceived my experiences with others as withholding love and acceptance. This energy intertwined itself into a tapestry of destructive thinking that evolved into negative emotions, thus giving birth to destructive behavior. My body would unconsciously tighten and hold onto accumulated energy with limited understanding of how to relax, release, or change how I viewed the world. I was perpetually stressed.

The past kept repeating itself, and suffering became a daily experience. I thought I was destined to live with sadness, anger and fear. It was the ability to become self-aware that allowed me to recognize that universal love is a metaphor for God — this is a gift bestowed to me and all of humankind.

If you want to discover the secret code to your life's purpose, start by looking back at your past. Ask yourself why certain experiences keep happening, and become a

"Life Watcher." Witness how you create your own story. Watch your thoughts appear and disappear. Notice how your emotions come and go. Feel how your body tightens and releases. Under the title "Notes to Me," record your observations and insights. These instructions will become the guidelines for discovering your own secret code that will identify your energetic pattern and the story and purpose of your life.

As William Shakespeare once said, "It is not in the stars that holds our destiny but in ourselves." When you become conscious of your patterns, this secret code is the key that unlocks your destiny.

Questions to Explore:

1. Are there circumstances in your life that keep repeating themselves?

2. How can you identify your energetic pattern and how might this affect your life story?

3. Do you know your life's purpose, and how may this affect your life?

Are You a Life Watcher?

I AM A "LIFE WATCHER." I watch, witness, observe and am aware of how each day begins and ends. I watch the progression of time that brings changes with the passing of years. I watch my heart beat, the movement of my breath, and how my thoughts come and go. I watch images appear and disappear, and emotions respond to self-expression and self-destruction. I watch the body modulate sensations. I watch how the sounds of harmony shift into dissonance. I watch the wounds of the ego manifest into patterns that repeat themselves. I watch as I accumulate insights as badges of wisdom. I watch relationships that come and go. I watch energy ebb and flow. I watch how the events of the outside world pulsate with its own rhythm. I ask questions with curiosity and watch the outcome. I watch how my intentions create my circumstances. I watch how I create my life with sacredness. I watch how my daily prayers feed my soul and connect me to my higher power.

Paying attention and being aware of your mind, body and emotions is a spiritual experience that ties you to something far greater than yourself. As a human in training, I recognize how my early wounds drive me to prove that I am okay, a good person who deserves love and validation. This quest drains my life force because I am stagnant with a repertoire of emotions that consists mostly of anger, self-loathing, sadness and fear. The anticipation of the future is a companion to worry about what might possibly be. Suffering means believing the chatter in my head and allowing my emotions to consume me.

When I watch how I protect my ego from being hurt, I am able to witness how this can also cause others to be hurt. It is the ability to sit, stand and lie in my brokenness that I discover a treasure that is beyond what words can describe. I realize that I am the author of my own life story.

Most of us will go to great lengths not to feel our initial wounds, or the emotions that are remnants from our past. Instead, we are distracted and preoccupied with avoiding pain. It is through this journey of avoidance and denial that we create our experiences to become the author of our one precious life.

Questions to Explore:

1. How do you escape from feeling the pain from your initial emotional wounds?

2. How has the avoidance of your suffering helped to create your life story?

When Does Personal Growth Begin?

I RECENTLY READ A MAGAZINE article about the renewed interest in Legos. Lego Mania is a revival that has entered the pop culture with the birth of Lego Clubs, Lego Stores, Lego Parties, and recent Lego films. Legos are rooted in nostalgia where there is a sweet recollection of timeless moments from childhood. There are some of us who are interested in the challenge of assembling elaborate Lego structures. These are people that focus on their cognition (their thinking mind) and the outcome. They live life in their head. Then there are others, like me, who are interested in building a sculpture based on creativity and expression of the soul. I am aware of my bodily sensations, thoughts and emotions, as I experiment with Legos. I practice the act of snapping, unsnapping and changing colors and shapes as an expression of my spiritual life. This process allows me to become more aware of my inner self — those thoughts and feelings that affect me and are co-mingled with the interactions of other people.

It is the evolution of the soul that is synonymous with personal growth. Self-actualization has become necessary to sustain life in modern times. Now, it is crucial that we are present in a way that supports the path of the soul. This pilgrimage is instrumental for those who want to evolve and develop the ability to remain in the present moment and connect to our higher self. Gary Zukav, an American spiritual teacher and author, known for the concept of aligning with the soul, says, "The requirements for our evolution have changed. Survival is no longer sufficient. Our evolution now requires us to develop spiritually — to align ourselves with the values of the soul — harmony, cooperation, sharing and reverence for life."

The late Jackie Robinson, who was the first African-American to play in the Major Baseball League, once said, "A life is not important except in the impact it has on other lives." His words speak the language of the soul. It begins with collaboration and the extension of helping hands as a symbol for love. This becomes a progression where life begins with the pronoun "I," grows with the Divine through "Thou," and universally becomes "Us," as a true definition of collective Love.

The passion to evolve is my life-long journey, connecting myself with others through the guidance of God. I have been a student of the mystical my entire life. The whole purpose of my questioning is based on my curiosity. The journey into the internal self-defines personal growth. I am reminded that feeling, expressing, not suppressing, and distinguishing between past and present emotions are all linked to being able to breathe into each present moment. From birth to adulthood, regulating our feelings means observing external stimuli, being attentive to our inner dialogue, watching physical pain and the unexpected, all as part of our pilgrimage. To pay homage to the ancient Greek aphorism, the meaning of life is found in the expression, "know thyself." So I observe my behaviors, such as compulsively eating instead of feeling my emotions. Or I watch my ego shift and become irritable, experience insomnia, or witness those thoughts that override the here and now. This is when I defer to the path of being a "Life Watcher."

Questions to Explore:

1. What kind of Lego builder are you? Are you focused on the details and outcome? Are you focused on the transformative process? Or maybe a little bit of both?

2. Has there been someone who has influenced your ability to spiritually transform?

3. Can you identify one or two incidents where you have influenced another person by contributing to their personal growth?

Is the Voice Inside Your
Head Your Friend?

A S A CHILD I remember standing next to the weeping willow tree in my backyard and blowing bubbles by dipping a wand into a bucket of soapy water. I watched with delight as they floated through space and faded into a mysterious unknown place. It felt like I was a magician with the power to make things appear and disappear, just like my thoughts.

We all have a voice in our head that speaks to us from within. No one else can hear it but you. In his book, *Untethered Soul: The Journey Beyond Yourself*, Michael Singer writes about that voice. He says, "We all have a mental dialogue that never stops talking and the majority of our thoughts have no relevance except to make you feel more comfortable with the world around us."

When we are focused on the present, our voice helps us to plan, organize, solve problems and gain wisdom from our higher self. This same voice, if left unsupervised, can hold us hostage to our past history or future fears. Have you asked yourself, "Is the voice inside my head my friend?"

Historically, my voice has not been my friend. I experienced a habituated thought pattern that served as protection from the external world. My head became filled with incessant talk that would expand and roar with judgment, worry and anger. When this occurs, my voice is not my friend, and I am left with thoughts and emotions that all point to the core belief of feeling unlovable. In contrast, I also recognize that there is a practical side to my voice that directs and enhances my being. Without this voice, I would never have functioned well in daily life.

Being able to observe your thoughts can alter your energy and guide your consciousness, helping you experience positive changes in your life.

Questions to Explore:

1. Is the voice in your head your friend or foe?

2. What do you notice about your voice? How does it help you or hinder you? Or has it been a little bit of both?

What Beliefs Are Creating
Your Life Story?

I N OUR CULTURE, KIDS who grow up experiencing a missing piece from childhood become grown-ups with emotional needs that remain frozen in time. Professionals may categorize the unmet desire to feel loved as pathology or an addict with a personality disorder. Maybe the true cause of this behavior stems from untouched, denied or avoided emotions that manifest later as fear, anger or grief. Unmet needs can create preconceived views about the world. For me, there is a thought pattern entrenched by three major beliefs — I am not lovable, I am not good enough, and no one cares about me — all rooted in unacknowledged emotions of grief, fear and anger. My feelings cluster together like branches from a tree that diverge into negativity, becoming the unconscious force that creates my story.

I once believed that happiness meant life would be as blissful as being able to eat decadent, rich food without gaining weight. I wanted a magic wand to manifest whatever I desired. Using my wand, I would wish away my suffering — those moments when I did not feel loved and protected, or when I did not receive my equal share of what I thought I deserved. This kept me in stagnation. It became evident that to become a real adult, I needed to re-parent myself in each moment of every day, giving myself what my mother could not provide.

Victor Frankl, a psychiatrist and Holocaust survivor, writes, "Everything can be taken from a man or woman but one thing: the last of human freedoms — to choose one's attitude in any given set of circumstances, to choose one's own way." This is possible by paying attention to what your body communicates and feeling your emotions as an avenue for re-parenting yourself.

How can adults who had difficult childhoods overcome their history to evolve and contribute their highest good to the world? Could it be possible that childhood wounds can become a blessing? As I write these thoughts, I am once again reminded that I am the author of my own life story, and I can create my heart's desire – and so can you. Anne Lamott, a well-known non-fiction writer, says, "Writing a Shitty First Draft (SFD) leads to clarity and sometimes brilliance in a second and third draft." I call my first story a draft, and no matter how many editions it takes, I will edit and rewrite my ongoing process to help me understand my own truth.

Questions to Explore:

1. What were the unmet needs from childhood that created the outline for your life story?

2. How can your adult self-re-parent you now?

How Can Universal Energy
Help Create Your Life?

I WAS A PASSENGER ON a bus traveling the hilly streets of San Francisco and asked the bus driver if it was difficult to navigate the congested streets. He said, "After working at this job for a while, I began to understand the rhythm and flow of the city, and I am now able to experience and anticipate the movement of energy that occurs throughout the day." I recognized that the bus driver was referring to the universal energy that surrounds life. It has a frequency essential to all living cells, whether human, animal or plant. If our movements are synchronized with the natural current that surrounds us, there is no resistance, and energy flows; resisting this energy, life becomes difficult.

Changing your life by accessing universal energy begins with the awareness of how your brain has patterns that create stories. This occurs during times when the brain focuses on incidents where there is emotional intensity, repetition, and the heightened focus that simultaneously works together. The stories human beings create develop because of beliefs about the self that become the filter to seeing our world. For example, if you believe that you are not good enough, and have no gifts to offer, this can potentially manifest into stories about self-loathing and loneliness. This hypothetical situation can build upon layers from past experiences to formulate repeated same-themed stories. When a script repeats itself, it becomes a belief that can be a barrier to spiritual growth, healing, and the life we desire.

One of the spiritual laws that governs our world and the entire cosmos is called the "Law of Attraction," which says we attract the things, events and people that come into our lives as an energetic vibration that has the potential to co-create our heart's desire. Negative energy attracts negative energy, and positive energy attracts positive energy. Thoughts, feelings and actions either produce positive or negative energy. What we focus on captures our attention and offers us the opportunity to become the author of our own life.

After I ask myself how universal energy can help re-create my own story, I realize the importance of changing what is no longer life enhancing, into a new inner dialogue that shifts my belief system. The inner dialogue now says, I have no limits – just possibilities and new stories that attach themselves to positive universal energy.

When the desired changes enter daily experiences, this movement makes room for edits to old stories, so that new ones can develop. We are putting on a new pair of glasses to see things differently. If you want to change your story, identify your strong beliefs by becoming aware of the repetition in your daily chatter. Pay attention to what you keep saying to yourself. For example, my self-talk surrounded feelings of incompetence and self-loathing, which later helped me recognize my entrenched beliefs — no one helps me, nothing I do works, and I am not enough. This awareness has facilitated new stories. I hold the lead role as the author of my life. When I see that I have been helped by others, that everything I do moves towards my own healing, and in the eyes of God, I am perfect as I am, my life evolves and transforms. I am responsible for helping my soul grow and expand.

Questions to Explore:

1. When you pay attention to the chatter in your head, what beliefs about self come into your present awareness?

2. Identify some possibilities for new stories that you want to create for your life.

Do You Have an
Energetic Pattern?

I HAVE MADE CHOICES IN the past out of anger. Not seething, violent anger, but rather the kind that silently seeps inside your soul and prevents you from thriving. Have you ever made decisions out of anger? For me, the anger is initiated from my past with the theme of not feeling loved.

My story began with adult role models who pointed their fingers with judgment and criticism. In retrospect, they were in their own pain. Original wounds hold energy patterns that take root and become an unconscious and entrenched part of oneself. I survived mine by fighting back. Not visibly like fighters in a boxing match or a fist-fight/hair-pulling event, but instead, as an insidious self-loathing that prevented me from feeling peace. No one noticed this, not even me. I was afraid, and like my original teachers, I interacted with the world by repeating the lessons that I was taught. This became the framework for a lifelong story similar to the cycle of violence — where the energy of everyday interactions builds until there is a release, and then the energy begins to rebuild again. It was as if I was asleep, and a thief entered through the window of my soul, stole my heart, and replaced it with the only thing I knew — a life of fear, grief and anger. I did not know that I was robbed of love.

This all seems so obvious – there is one story which keeps repeating itself throughout an adult life. An example of this is reflected in the 1993 movie called *Groundhog Day*, starring Bill Murray and Andie MacDowell. Murray plays an egocentric Pittsburgh TV weatherman, named Phil Connors, who covers the annual Groundhog Day event. He finds himself in a time loop, where he awakens to the same day, with the opportunity to change, and cannot escape until he alters his behavior.

The irony is that most of us have a pattern that the ego creates to avoid hurt. Have you ever wondered why you may find yourself in certain situations repeatedly? For instance, do you enter relationships with the same type of person and wonder why it does not work? Or maybe you find jobs where you experience frequent interpersonal conflict? You may have even asked yourself, "Why do certain external situations keep happening to me?" It happens because there is an energetic pattern, an unconscious belief about self that keeps repeating itself. For example, Bill Murray's character had no empathy for others, believing that people existed for the sole purpose of being of service to him. I believe when awareness of your beliefs comes into consciousness, you can change the energetic pattern of your life.

Questions to Explore:

1. What repetitive patterns do you experience that make you wonder why certain things keep happening to you?

2. Has the energetic pattern you've created become a barrier to experiencing love, joy and peace?

Can Change Promote Transformation?

WALKING THROUGH THE PARK, I see dandelions — bright flowers popping out of green grass that capture a moment in time. It does not matter to me that they are weeds, as it is a delightful snapshot. The image reminds me that nature is temporary, as are the seasons, plant cycles and the animal kingdom. Everything has its own cyclical movement which becomes a manifestation of a mystical prayer rooted in sacredness, beyond words.

There is something about this constant movement that allows us to see, feel and experience this evolution. When we are birthed into our physical bodies, and travel along the developmental stages of personhood, everything around and within us changes. During our journey, we choose a path that is often not conscious, but somehow deeply rooted in the familiar. By this I mean that a limited repertoire of personal awareness is developed that becomes the theme of one's life. It is as if our thoughts, emotions and body sensations become as comfortable as old slippers. Therefore, I used to wish that everything and everyone around me would remain the same. I would tell myself that I hated change and intentionally resisted acknowledging the bigger picture. My energy would become blocked as I unconsciously did not allow it to move. But over time, I learned that the key is to just allow the current to flow, like the waves in the ocean that ebb and flow.

Change is part of a natural progression that fosters transformation. We evolve when there is a conscious choice to focus on emotional and spiritual development. Leo Tolstoy said, "Everyone thinks of changing the world, but no one thinks of changing himself." All living things on this planet are connected to their own cycle. As human beings, this cycle occurs when there is a willingness to receive whatever presents itself during our lifespan, along with a commitment to recognize the strength we possess. This is defined as resiliency — having the capacity to foster one's inner flexibility by accessing our natural gifts. This has personally helped give meaning, insight and comfort to what, at times, has felt disheartening. I take inventory of my own resilience by creating a love for learning, the passion for cultivating the growth of my soul and relationship with God, the ability to see the metaphors and paradoxes of life, and insight into the complexity of human dynamics.

Questions to Explore:

To understand the evolution of your life, take inventory of your own resilience and then explore the following questions:

1. How has resiliency helped your spiritual evolution?

2. What changes in your life have you resisted and what have you transformed?

Can You Let Go of Your Story and Create Something New?

W E ALL HAVE A story to tell, one which often holds the roots of our family tree. The unfolding of life's events is like origami, the art of paper folding – transforming flat, square sheets of paper into works of art. These altered shapes represent symbols and unique descriptions of the tribulations and triumphs that re-tell the narratives of our lives.

When a story keeps repeating, self-reflection becomes the soil for personal growth. You may ask the question, "Why does this keep happening to me?" Becoming aware of your own story and its patterns provides an opportunity to release the past and create something new. American director and producer Steven Spielberg said, "People have forgotten how to tell a story. Stories don't have a middle or an end. They usually have a beginning that never stops beginning."

The truth is that our thoughts and emotions are repetitive, creating the same narrative. How we feel about a situation and how others respond is a daily reality. I recently had a former mid-school student contact me via Facebook. She wanted to tell me about her struggles to be successful and to share a memory of the day her teacher requested that she leave the classroom due to her behavior. When I saw her standing in the hallway looking upset, I invited her into my office to talk about her version of this incident. I did not realize the impact I had on this student until I received her message years later. Her perceptions of the event attributed much more importance than I understood, showing me that kindness can become life changing. It is our thoughts that create the experiences of human drama – those markers that consist of people, places, plots, conflicts and resolutions. These become the language that gives birth to a belief system.

My past stories are tales of being hyper vigilant, always scanning for my safety from judgment and criticism, with the desire to feel nurtured. I did not love myself, and so I looked for validation in all the wrong places. It was my "heart" that was the theme for the stories of my life. These emotional experiences, if integrated as felt-energy, can become the gift of presence manifesting as peace, joy and love.

To help understand the importance of emotional intelligence, awareness and integration of feelings, the Institute of Heart Math, an educational organization led by Doc Childre, has developed user-friendly tools to help individuals gain personal balance, insight and fulfillment. Based on their research, "Heart rhythms stand out as the most reflective of inner emotional states. Negative emotions lead to an increase in the autonomic nervous system that adversely affects the whole body." The stories human beings create are often frozen, unintegrated emotions.

Michael Brown, author of *The Presence Process*, says, "Unresolved emotional memories from childhood become the triggered events from daily life that provide opportunities to resolve stored negative emotions." He further states, "As long as we feel we have separate physical bodies, brains, emotional and vibratory bodies, there is a gap between ourselves and all others. This gap becomes even more prevalent when we try to control our emotions or project them on to others by blaming them." Not being able to integrate our feelings is what may be a barrier to creating a new story and may explain the prevalence of addictions in society.

There are some who say that our single purpose is for our soul to evolve and that part of our growth is to accept whatever life presents. We grow when we create a new story for our life, just like flowers that bloom into their own magnificence. Rumi, a thirteenth century poet and Sufi Mystic wrote, "This being human is a guest house. Every morning is a new arrival. A joy, a depression, a meanness, some momentary awareness comes as an unexpected visitor...Welcome and entertain them all. Treat each guest honorably. The dark thought, the shame, the malice, meet them at the door laughing, and invite them in. Be grateful for whoever comes, because each has been sent as a guide from beyond."

Questions to Explore:

1. What is the story that keeps repeating itself in your life?

2. What challenging emotions do you experience regularly?

Do You Ever Get Angry?

ANGER IS A FEELING that catches my attention. It is an energy that manifests in many different forms. Anger can be seen as acts of violence, felt as words that hurt, expressed in negative thinking, or by the mere act of withholding love. Being an initiator or a recipient of anger can rob you of your well-being. We can acknowledge its destructiveness and make changes, or we can become anesthetized by these very actions. Its powers are significant and can leave you with feelings of helplessness, or the inability to solve problems. Anger can manifest itself into avoidance, blame, shame, self-loathing and grief. Yet, it can also be a motivating force to succeed against all odds.

Anger is rooted in the core beliefs that we have about ourselves. These are the formulated perceptions that tell the stories from our past and foster the fear that comes from anticipating the future. We filter the world through these thoughts with the same kind of fluidity as the seasons when they change. My own anger begins with automatic hyper vigilance, scanning for safety. I ask myself, "Am I being judged as not good enough? Am I being labeled as unlovable? Am I being told that I can't have something that I want?"

Mildred Norman Ryder, also known as "Peace Pilgrim" (www.peacepilgrim.org), is a role model for teaching humankind how to be free from anger and live in peace. She was a modern-day sage who lived in simplicity and spiritual faith as she walked across America for 28 years speaking about peace. She said, "On the anger habit: Do not suppress it – it will hurt your inside. Do not express it, this would not hurt your inside, it would cause ripples in your surroundings. The question is what can you do to transform your anger?" First, feel it without hurting yourself or someone else. It is important to learn from and integrate these feelings and distinguish yourself between being a victim of your anger and being empowered by it.

Develop the following strategies:

- Increase your self-awareness by paying attention to what you are thinking and feeling. "If you realized how powerful your thoughts are, you would never think a negative thought."
  ~ *Peace Pilgrim*

- Remind yourself not to take everything that other people do so personally. "When you find peace within yourself, you become the kind of person who can live with others."
  ~ *Peace Pilgrim*

- Focus your thoughts by letting go and letting God. "Awaken the divine nature that is within."
  ~ *Peace Pilgrim*

- Have compassion for the hurt and pain that others feel. "Before the tongue can speak, it must have lost the power to wound."
  ~*Peace Pilgrim*

Questions to Explore:

To begin to understand if anger affects your life, ask yourself:

1. How often do I feel angry?

2. What makes me feel angry?

3. What are some of the strategies I have developed to help manage my anger?

How Can I Learn to Forgive Myself and Others?

F ORGIVENESS IS THE KEY to obtaining inner peace. When we do not forgive, we will not thrive. Scripture says, "And whenever you stand up to pray, if you have something against anyone, forgive so that your Father in heaven may forgive you your wrongdoings."*(Mark 11:25, Common English Bible)*. Human beings are not perfect, and thus, it is necessary to view each other with mercy. Most faiths believe that making amends is necessary for achieving inner clemency.

The Hidden Power of the Heart is written by Sara Paddison, who writes about the interplay between the heart and brain and its effect on overall health. She says, "Sincere forgiveness isn't colored with expectations that the other person apologizes or changes. Don't worry whether they finally understand you. Love them and release them. Life feeds back truth to people in its own way and time."

Research supports the idea that concealing negativity within the heart can damage our overall health. Harboring resentments are reflected in both our thoughts and negative emotional patterns which influence the entire body's systems. Chronic emotional states such as anger, fear, and grief lead to dissonance, and affect the autonomic nervous system, hormonal and immune system, the heart and the brain. The benefits of forgiveness offer positive outcomes for mental, physical, emotional and spiritual health.

Archbishop Desmond Tutu, leading human rights activist from Cape Town, South Africa, and Nobel Prize recipient, wrote *The Book of Forgiving*. In it, he says that the steps to forgiving and healing require the telling of the story, naming the hurt, granting forgiveness, and renewing or releasing the relationship in question.

There are additional frameworks for forgiveness that are universal:

- Acknowledging the incident that caused the pain.
- Understanding that relief from the event is a process.
- Deciding that you are ready to let go of feeling like a victim, and moving on with life.
- Reframing the incident by trying to understand the perpetrator's side of the story.
- Shifting your perspective of this event to one that builds inner wisdom.

For me, not being able to forgive myself has been a barrier to living life fully. My negative feelings associated with the interactions of others, I often took personally. The reactions to external situations instigated regret, remorse, blame, shame, and self-hatred. I would feel unlovable and automatically look for proof to validate this belief. Now, I find myself wishing for a "do-over," or a second chance to repent.

I realize that this needs to occur with introspection guided by my heartfelt desire to forgive and change my perceptions. Self-forgiveness is something that is often not acknowledged as a passage towards redemption.

The late Norman Cousins, a journalist and world peace advocate, said, "Life is an adventure in forgiveness." This pearl of wisdom can be interpreted as part of the soul's journey.

Questions to Explore:

1. How do I forgive myself and how do I not forgive myself?

2. How might compassion and forgiveness help to forgive those who have hurt me?

How Do I Give Away My
Personal Power?

P OWER IS DEFINED AS having the ability to act or produce an effect on something or someone. Most human beings want power. Many of us believe we can control how people think, act or feel. The desire to govern others is widespread and can be perceived as an attempt to feel safe from our deepest fears. Often, however, we do not manifest what we want, which leads to feelings of disempowerment. We may dream of being a protagonist in a modern-day fairy tale with magical powers to fulfill our heart's desires. Elizabeth Gilbert, in her book, *Eat, Pray, Love: One Woman's Search for Everything Across Italy, India and Indonesia*, says, "I met an old lady once, almost a hundred years old, and she told me, there are only two questions that human beings have ever fought over all through history. How much do you love me? And who's in charge?"

I have heard people say, "Don't give away your power." What you believe and feel about yourself gives birth to victimhood and the opportunity to lose your power. The act of feeling, expressing, acknowledging and letting go of emotions can influence personal power. The opposite of giving away your power is the ability to love yourself. This means having an inner voice programmed for self-compassion, and empathy for yourself and others. Making conscious choices and responding, instead of reacting, to external circumstances helps us to feel empowered.

"Owning our story and loving ourselves through that process is the bravest thing that we'll ever do," writes Brené Brown, an American scholar and researcher. In her book, *The Hustle for Worthiness*, she describes "P words" as those that involve such behaviors as pleasing, perfecting, pretending, and proving. People pleasing comes with the desire to be liked and accepted. Perfectionism accompanies the need to feel competent, reinforcing self-worth. Pretending is not accepting situations or circumstances. Proving one's self is an avenue for feeling personally sanctioned as adequate.

I have familiarity with the negative effects of "P words" in my life. I have pleased others at my own expense with the hope of being paid with love. Trying to be perfect allowed my inner critic to reinforce my feelings of incompetence and self-worth. I pretended and lied to myself about who I was in order to be consistent with my story. I wanted to prove that I was okay. I gave the outside world my power, and allowed my self-worth to be measured by others. I have since come to the realization that our beliefs must be internally driven and not reliant on external sources.

We create our lives by our self-beliefs, and we can change our own stories from disempowered to empowered. This means you must be aware of the effects of "P words" by asking those questions that promote self-awareness. Am I people pleasing? Is my self-worth fragile? Am I trying to prove that I am okay? Am I allowing others to measure my worth? When

I am behaving negatively, do I feel powerless? Am I being judgmental so I can feel better about myself?

These queries are instrumental in affecting change in our lives. Ask the questions of empowerment, and then observe the behaviors that encourage an outcome that positively affect how you use your personal power.

Questions to Explore:

1. How do I give away my power?

2. If you allow others to affect your personal power, how does "hustling for your worthiness" affect your life story?

How Are You Resilient?

WHEN LIFE PRESENTS ITS many challenges, the proverbial phrase, "When the world gives you lemons, make lemonade," comes to mind. And although this is a common cultural truth, I find myself asking, "What defines the ability to take something as sour as adversity and turn it into the sweetness of inner strength?" The answer to this question resides in resiliency — the ability to pick yourself up and keep moving forward during difficult times.

Our life experiences are the teachers that model how to stand strong and tall. I remember one of my work colleagues confiding in me that as a child her parents would constantly argue and drink. She did not understand what loving relationships looked or felt like until she started watching television sitcoms. I shared a similar experience — my parents were not emotionally present. They were always working, and when they came home, they were tired, overwhelmed, and unavailable. Although I know they were doing their very best, I often felt lonely and would hang out with my friends at their homes to experience healthy family interactions.

Both my friend and I were robust and able to adapt to our family situations, while still finding ways to get our needs met. Being resilient is both a process and skill that requires practice and a shift in mindset, one that is strong and hardy like weeds that sustain themselves in inclement weather.

When we become adults without having the opportunity to develop the skills necessary to sustain relationships and cope with life's challenges, we can still cultivate resiliency by practicing awareness. Resiliency is the ability to pay attention to our feelings and thoughts and not allow them to disrupt the flow of our lives. It is through trial and error that we learn to create our own strategies for making lemonade, one that quenches our thirst and offers relief.

Questions to Explore:

1. Did anyone teach you to be resilient? If so, what do you remember about what you learned?

2. Are there any situations in your life where you have had the inner strength to pick yourself up and bounce right back?

How Can Feeling Broken
Manifest Hope?

M Y SOUL AND PHYSICAL body were birthed into the twentieth century in a moment in time. It was an ordinary day, where the past and present were entwined with the trajectory of my future. I was born into a family where my female ancestors wanted their children to receive the love that they felt they did not have. Believing they were helping their offspring to survive, they were judgmental and critical. This was passed on through my lineage, and unconsciously manifested into perfectionism giving me the desire to numb my feelings of unworthiness with food.

I unconsciously chose to go on the pilgrimage described by the late Joseph Campbell in the mythology of *Hero's Journey*, wherein a volunteer goes out on behalf of the tribe. I was that volunteer, facing danger and making self-sacrifices to bring love into the light.

The twists and turns of the journey helped to transform my feelings of brokenness and became the impetus for a resolution of a lineage of women not able to nurture themselves. As part of my own development, I lived and meditated with feelings of being broken. I went on this adventure in search of love, discovering that this universal truth is synonymous with God, and love is an open-ended story. It is the exchange of energy-in-motion, reflected in our social communication, both by non-verbal cues and chosen words highlighted by the intonation of our voices.

Bert Hellinger, German psychologist and founder of the Family Constellation Model, said, "Many of us unconsciously 'take on' destructive familial patterns as a way of belonging." This theory helps us to understand these patterns as moments of self-insight that can create a new life course.

Growing up, despair was ingrained in the roots of my family. Although their intention was to share and pass on life's abundance, there were unseen tiny crevasses of hidden pain that went unacknowledged. In the novel, *The Salt Garden*, author Cindy McCormick Martinusen describes my ancestors, "I see the fragmented beauty of grace in their lives despite continued struggles. Beautiful mosaics formed by broken pieces." I believe that jagged, round and sheared bits of broken glass are the salvation that can transform the darkness into light. Families bring with them both anguish and hope. I have come to believe that hope and optimism reside within our brokenness.

Anais Nin, the late American writer and diarist, defined the interaction between the ego and the soul by saying, "We do not grow absolutely, chronologically. We grow sometimes in one dimension, and not in another; unevenly. We grow partially. We are relative. We are mature in one realm, childish in another. The past, present, and future mingle and pull us backward, forward, or fix us in the present. We are made up of layers, cells, constellations." This statement describes the energetic fields that connect us to each other through love, allowing us to look beneath the layers of anger, fear and sorrow to offer us hope.

There are many families that are broken, and our awareness of their moments of hopelessness can help us become compassionate with each other. Poet and writer C. JoyBell says, "A broken soul is not the absence of beauty, but a cracked and torn soul reeks of the sweet incense it contains."

Without the gift of the brokenness of my family, and my willingness to face my fears with introspection and awareness, I would not have become the person that I am today, and for this I am grateful.

Questions to Explore:

1. Is there any part of your inner self that feels broken that may be rooted in the constellation of your family?

2. What beauty can be found in those broken pieces that can be assembled to create a beautiful mosaic in your life?

How Can You Surrender the
Burdens of Your Heart?

W HAT WEIGHS HEAVILY ON your heart is all part of
the human experience. To be alive means there are
many opportunities for fear to highjack your inner-peace or
an illness to rob you of your well-being. No one is immune
to the hurt that accompanies physical pain, sorrow or anger.
When life pushes us to our knees, the collective wisdom of
most religions tells us to surrender our burdens and acquiesce
in faith. It is the ability to trust that allows harmony, joy and
love to enter our lives.

Rumi, a thirteenth century Sufi poet and mystic, wrote
a poem called "A Necessary Autumn Inside Each" that tells
us that spiritual growth occurs when we are willing to let
go. He says, "There is a necessary dying, and then Jesus is
breathing again. Very little grows on jagged rock. Be ground.
Be crumbled, so wildflowers will come up where you are.
You've been stony for too many years. Try something
different. Surrender."

For some, being able to surrender is difficult. Many of
us don't know how to let go, and, when we try, we are often
hesitant to believe transformation can occur. Tosha Silver,

author of the book, *Outrageous Openness*, instructs us on how to surrender the burdens of the heart. She says to create a "God Box" by putting a one-word message inside as a symbol of letting go and letting God. So I write LOVE and place it inside.

In her second book, *Change Me Prayers*, she tells us to surrender through prayer. So I pray, "Change me, Divine Beloved, and help me to let go of my past. Fill my heart with love as a sacrament that symbolizes my vision of goodness in self and in others." When I think of the word LOVE held in my God box, and recite my letting-go prayer, strong emotions arise and I surrender. My heart feels unencumbered and more responsive to whatever life presents. Then miraculously, there is a crack, a slight opening between my ego and spirit that gradually releases the burdens held within.

Questions to Explore:

1. What burdens do you hold in your heart?

2. What word would you place in your God Box and what prayer would help to surrender to your hurting heart?

Is a Wound from Your Past
Stopping Your Chi?

THE ANCIENT CHINESE BELIEVE in chi, the fundamental energy connecting all things, as an unfolding of reality. This natural order and rhythm makes life dynamic, as energy flows by expanding and contracting and uniting as one.

I have witnessed my own inner psyche fight over whether I am friend or foe to myself. I have responded to this inner conflict by tensing my body with the anticipation of being emotionally attacked. This energetic pattern has followed me from childhood.

As I watch my consciousness, I sense an opportunity to choose between contracting and expanding my energy. These feelings are accompanied by the sensation of a roller coaster as it ascends and descends into screaming voices.

Going from fear to love and back again, human beings experience a continuum of emotions. When I allow this energy to move through me, I can accept whatever occurs without judgment. I feel free. The poet, Marie Tavorges Stilkind, best describes this same observation when she says, "Today I know that I cannot control the ocean tides. I can only go with the flow. When I struggle, and try to organize the Atlantic to my specifications, I sink. If I flail and thrash and growl and grumble, I go under. But if I let go and float, I am borne aloft." I believe that we can choose either to "go with the flow" or to block our own energy. Chronic contraction breeds conflict, and expansion creates harmony.

As part of a daily ritual, join me and expand your life force by becoming more aware of your energy flow. With each breath, practice letting go of whatever gets in the way of experiencing peace, love and joy in your life.

Questions to Explore:

1. How is a wound from the past stopping the flow of your energy?

2. What do you notice when you expand or contract your energy?

How Does Your Body
Communicate with You?

MANY OF US KNOW that life creates a story — one that holds cellular memories in our bodies as well as in our minds and spirit. The body stores and archives the past as history, recording events as if it were a computer. It reports back what is occurring from moment to moment. Transformation and health happen by developing an internal life that focuses on feedback from our bodies. The body communicates to us through an internal map that is programmed for survival, safety, and a sense of well-being.

The late Martha Graham, a twentieth century dancer, known for creating the language of movement, said, "The body never lies." It tells us when it is hurt, hungry, thirsty, in pain, tired, scared and emotionally imbalanced. It has an alarm system that communicates when danger is present. When under stress, the fight/flight response is the mechanism that helps us to survive. When we pay attention to the body's sensations, there is a physiological response that is alerted to danger and unique to the individual. These signs have varied symptoms such as sweating, rapid breathing, a flushed face, an inner voice that cries "run," a heart that pounds, muscles that tighten, and a jaw that clinches.

Gabor Mate, MD, physician and author of the book, *When the Body Says No — Exploring the Stress-Disease Connection,* says, "The mind and body are inseparable, in that illness and health cannot be understood in isolation from the life histories, social context, and emotional patterns of human beings."

Furthermore, there is an interconnection between whole body intelligence and the body's ability to respond to danger. A frequent occurrence in the modern world is to lose touch with this warning system. The more prevalent silent stressor has now become emotional, which is a shift from the survival needs of our ancestors. In our present culture, we often either ignore, become hyper-alert, or try to suppress or control our feelings. We are not taught how to recognize, feel or handle emotions, and many of us can't distinguish what we are feeling. The physiology of stress wears down our bodies because we have not developed the competence to recognize or experience our emotions.

Dr. Mate, says, "Emotional competence requires the capacity to feel and express our emotions, to be able to distinguish between the present and the past, and not to repress feelings for the sake of acceptance." This means we need to consciously be aware of our emotional state, be cognizant of its effect on others, and observe the physiological changes in our nervous system, hormones and immune system. The ability to self-regulate emotions is being able to acknowledge, identify and feel the emotion, and breathe into these feelings with the felt sensation of presence. Developing emotional competence has positive implications for managing stress and having good health.

As my own story evolved, there were a few life experiences where my survival was in jeopardy. Thankfully, my body quickly responded and told me that I was in danger. I have come to understand that a lot of my stress was linked to emotional competence. My fear of rejection, not believing I was good enough, and feeling unlovable – all have been key stressors linked to the past. These three themes of victimhood became a repeated life story. It was time to let go of these old beliefs and my victimhood status.

Now, when the emotions of fear, grief and anger are present, I breathe and feel the feelings often emanating from the heart. Then I pay attention to my bodily sensations and how they change in each moment. I watch my body shift from the sympathetic to parasympathetic nervous system and observe the miracle of our innate ability to self-regulate and rebalance.

Questions to Explore:

1. How does your body communicate chronic physical and emotional conditions?

2. How do your emotions affect your ability to manage chronic stress?

3. What steps have you taken to manage your stress?

How Can Breathing Help You Cope with Life's Challenges?

THERE IS A SANSKRIT proverb that says, "For breath is life, and if you breathe well you will live long on earth." Breath is also known as "prana," a vital energy that enters the body through our cells and circulatory system. This is called "conscious breathing" in Western culture, which is considered vital energy having positive effects on our thoughts and emotions, as well as other health benefits such as blood pressure regulation, stress management, and control over anxiety.

Our breathing is hardwired through our sympathetic and parasympathetic nervous systems. When we are in a flight/fight response, rapid breathing can be lifesaving. Slow, deliberate breathing can deepen the ability to relax and experience a restful sleep. Breathing can also be an avenue to connect us with our inner self, offering a sanctuary of bliss. Breathing fully and easily is a life pleasure. If our breath ceases, life as we know it, stops.

When we are conscious of our breathing, we inhale and exhale more deeply, allowing for the space between breaths. It becomes a whole body rhythmic experience. Like the ebb and flow of the ocean, we experience the respiratory waves of breath. Miraculously, our body has its own pulse that adjusts to what is occurring within our body and in our environment.

All animals on earth live in an ocean of air. After a period of practicing conscious breathing techniques, it occurred to me that in any given second, my breath could become an inner resource that could be accessed whenever I needed to calm myself. It is conscious breathing that allows me to surrender to whatever is occurring at any moment.

My breath, like the ocean, has a flow that seems mysterious. With practice, I learned to surrender to my conscious breath, giving way to an inner arsenal that equips me to meet life's challenges. This gift helps me become a better mother to that little girl that still lives inside of me. When I inhale and exhale my deepest fears, anger and grief, I let go and surrender to the natural cadence of life.

Questions to Explore:

1. In what ways might you practice conscious breathing?

2. How does your breathing affect your life?

In What Ways Do You
Have an Inner Life?

A N INNER LIFE IS a sacrament of devotion that requires a daily practice made up of rituals that commit to repetition. Following a ceremony of prayer helps to develop abundance — one that is in harmony with the flow of love. It is with this offering of reverence that I invite God into my heart with a deep surrender and the release of attachment to any outcome.

My ritual begins with setting an intention for the day. I think about the kind of goodness I would like to manifest. This often is a reminder to love myself. Then I say a prayer of surrender by asking God to work through me and affirm my trust and belief in the highest good. Next, I become a "Life Watcher," and observe my energy and those around me. I watch if my energy comingles with others and how this may create a different type of energetic pattern. I pay attention to my thoughts and emotions and experience what my body is communicating to me. When my body tells me that I am off-balance, I ask for help and continue to allow the evolution of the day to unfold. I take inventory of my blessings and offer gratitude for these gifts by acknowledging them in a journal.

Over time, I notice that my gratitude list becomes longer, and my energy shifts to one of deep appreciation and wealth that goes beyond the material realm. I respond to this manifestation by offering gestures of kindness to myself and others. As the story of each day develops, I feel my soul expand and my anguish disappear. My inner life then becomes an energetic practice that navigates back and forth between my ego and my soul.

Questions to Explore:

1. In what ways do you have an inner life that helps you celebrate and meet the challenges of daily living?

2. What rituals feed your soul to providing daily sustenance?

In What Ways Are You an Artist?

"Bonfire"
by Mary-Beth Klastorin, Age 8

The flickering flames of burning leaves,
Red, yellow, and blue.
The crackling sounds of a bonfire
The burning ashes playing in the air
The hot flames of bonfire
The wood crackling
The flames of a bonfire are pretty at night.

I DISCOVERED INNER WEALTH THAT went beyond my imagination when the poem "Bonfire" entered back into my life. It was a forgotten part of my past. This gift did not come to me until a family member discovered a box filled with papers that were buried and archived as history. Within this box lay dormant the expression of an eight-year-old little girl who wrote poetry symbolizing the bridge between ego and soul.

We are all artists who create our daily lives by how we work, play, and relate to others. Don Miguel Ruiz, author of *The Four Agreements,* says, "We express our art in everything we say, everything we feel, and everything we do. The creation is ongoing, it is endless, it is happening in every moment."

I believe that we are all artists expressing our inner world by what we see and feel. The ability to self-create is a gift we give to ourselves and others.

Questions to Explore:

1. Do you think that your creativity is reflected in the way you think, how you see the world, or in your ability to express yourself?

2. How are you an artist, and what do you long to create for yourself and the world?

How Do Emotions Affect You?

E MOTIONS COME FROM DEEP within, emerging from mood, circumstances or relationships. Emotions can also be words that inspire or inhibit personal growth. An emotion can produce images that embrace our hearts, shift our thinking, and affect our physical bodies. Anger, sadness and fear are some of the emotions that create feelings, and feelings have been the narrative of my life story.

Throughout my life, anger would often flare. I would muster an attitude that left no space for kindness or empathy towards anyone, including myself. At its core were feelings of not being accepted or loved. The voice inside my head would say, "I don't care. It doesn't matter." But I did care, and it did matter. I was unaware of how this emotion elicited apathy, subsequently affecting my relationships in a negative way. There have been many stories in my life created with the same theme.

For me, sadness is a leftover childhood remnant. I did not feel loved, and this created regular heartbreak that left tiny pieces of grief and an aching desire to feel whole. When I became conscious of the possibility that self-love lay dormant in my heart, I felt motivated to learn how to love myself. During this process, I remember placing notes all around my house as a reminder: "I am nurturing myself like I would my own child." "I am focusing on my inner life to create balance and harmony." "When I am grateful, this becomes an avenue for my own transformation." These notes were the inspiration for "Spirit Fortunes," the cards I created to foster loving energy in daily life.

Fear is a barrier to getting in touch with my feelings. I frequently felt that if I revealed my true self, the world would discover that I was not good enough. My body would scream out for me to pay attention to what I was feeling. It spoke to me with a clinched jaw, a rapid heartbeat, or a shallow breath, but I chose to ignore the messages.

Now, when I realize that fear is holding me back, I become more conscious of my whole body. I pay attention to what my physical self is communicating. I notice that when anger, sadness and fear are absent, the voice inside my head becomes silent. I feel peace and can experience the pulse and rhythm of my life. I learn that emotions are not intended to be stored in our bodies. But rather, emotions are energy that require a felt experience that is meant to be released.

Questions to Explore:

1. What repeated emotion helps to create the stories of your life?

2. Are you afraid to feel your emotions, and if you are, what do you do to avoid your feelings?

How Do You Love Yourself?

M OST OF US WANT more love in our lives. Often, love is synonymous with having a romantic relationship, and the celebration of Valentine's Day. The innate desire to pair off with another is a natural urge for the continuation of our species. However, before experiencing a connection with a mate, it is important to love oneself first. Self-love occurs when we progressively learn to unconditionally accept ourselves. It is what contributes to having a basic belief in our own goodness that builds space for our inner self to thrive. Self-love is both developed and modeled during infancy and early childhood by our initial attachment figures, and that progresses well into the adolescent years.

We develop self-love by looking at our lives as an artist does when painting on blank paper. Watch how the choice of colors affect how we feel. The subtleties of hues allow us to observe how love blends in an array of emotions to become a magnificent rainbow. Aberjhani, author of *Journey through the Power of the Rainbow*, calls upon all of us to "Dare to love yourself as if you were a rainbow with gold at both ends."

When you love yourself, emotions blend into colors that fill our inner self with love. Matthew 22:37-39 (King

James Version of the Bible, 1611) tells us, "You shall love the Lord your God with all your heart and with all your soul and with all your mind. You shall love your neighbor as yourself."

Self-love is the work of the soul promoting emotional and spiritual balance. Beau Taplin, author of *The Wild Heart*, a collection of poems and short stories, said, "Self-love is an ocean and your heart is a vessel. Make it full, and any excess will spill over into the lives of the people you hold dear. But you must come first." Only when we appreciate our evolution into a self-actualized individual, can we have a loving relationship with another.

When I express my emotions with watercolors on canvas, I watch love emerge. I remember that when I love myself, feelings of emptiness cease. I listen to my inner voice whisper love songs written for me. I watch self-love evolve into self-care. Saying encouraging words to myself helps me to believe I am lovable. I make choices for my highest good. I know love is in my heart when I stop thinking about what I don't have, and acknowledge my blessings.

Questions to Explore:

1. In what ways do you express your love for self?

2. How does the ability to love yourself affect the ways love is created in your life?

What Do You Crave?

THERE ARE DAYS WHEN I need something sweet, and I search for a bakery that showcases eclairs stuffed with pastry cream and iced with thick chocolate. Other times, I just want to buy a new outfit even though I have a closet full of clothes. This describes my craving, a wanting that pops up unexpectedly like a jack-in-the-box. As I practice being a "Life Watcher" and observe myself, I witness how my cravings often coincide with feeble attempts to numb, deny, or push away emotions.

This same intense energy will not allow me to ignore the wish for a magic wand, one that can grant my every desire. The truth is, when I ask my deepest self what I crave, my inner voice answers, "What you really crave are not sweets that often numb you or more clothes to distract you from your true feelings. Instead, your deepest desire is to love and be loved."

In my core is the need for love for myself and in my relationships – and for all of my actions to be loving. Love becomes my creation, and my soul inhales and exhales my deepest desire to be filled with the presence of love. Jodi Picoult, author of *Handle with Care*, says, "What we all want, really, is to be loved. That craving drives our worst behavior." I have seen my own vilest behavior – the kind that is mean, angry, and even vindictive – when I don't feel loved. These are the times when I perceive myself as being judged. Whether this is imagined or real, what I see, feel and experience has the same message — I am not lovable, ricocheting back to my feeling unworthy. This is when I want to wave my magic wand — one, two, three times – and like a magician, create what seems impossible. *Poof,* compassion for self and others is felt. *Poof,* my greatest assets are apparent. *Poof,* peace permeates the air as if fairy dust sprinkles a trail of glitter and illuminates the way back to my heart. I am reminded that we all deserve to feel love, be loved, and give love – for that is where God lives.

As Buddha said, "You can search throughout the entire universe for someone who is more deserving of your love and affection than you are yourself, and that person is not to be found anywhere. You yourself, as much as anybody in the entire universe deserve your love and affection."

Questions to Explore:

1. If you had a magic wand, what would you wish for in your life?

2. When you crave something, what emotions coincide with your cravings?

In What Ways Are You Addicted to Something?

ADDICTION IS DEFINED AS a persistent, compulsive dependence on a behavior or substance. It is said there are two types of addiction: substance addiction and process addiction. Substance addiction is a dependency on drugs, alcohol, compulsive eating, or cigarettes. Process addiction refers to the chronic obsession to take part in certain activities or behaviors, such as gambling, internet and sex. Our incomplete thoughts, emotions and internal sanctions of our bodies develop an energetic pattern behind our obsessive behaviors and contribute to the habits of addiction.

Many years ago, I discovered that food could alter my biochemistry. When I would eat carbohydrates such as bread, cookies, or chocolate, I noticed my mood shift and my emotions become numb, at least for a little while. So I developed the habit of seeking solace in food. I would eat when I was angry, afraid, sad or even happy. Food felt like it was a carbohydrate party on a platter calling my name. This displaced excessive eating promotes inflammation in my body, affecting my physical and mental health. This type of behavior can develop into digestive problems, diabetes, heart disease, or cancer.

Overeating was a destructive force in my life that caused me to suffer. When I would become aware of my thoughts and feel my emotions, things changed

Addictions cause suffering to self and others, but can transform into personal growth. This does not occur through happiness and joy, but through the failure and rejection that follow as a consequence. Father Richard Rohr, a teacher of Christian mysticism, says, "If you don't transform your suffering, you will transmute. Suffering occurs when we don't get what we want or do not accept what is." When we are aware of ourselves and others, we acknowledge our light and manifest our magnificence by letting go and accepting life as it unfolds.

Questions to Explore:

1. What obsessive thoughts and feelings interfere with experiencing love, joy and peace in your life?

2. Do you have an addiction that causes suffering to yourself and others?

How Do You Cultivate
Gratitude in Your Daily Life?

G RATITUDE IS DEFINED AS the state of being grateful and thankful. As each day unfolds, I look for opportunities to be grateful and notice that there is a shift in the richness of my spiritual life and physical health.

Dr. Robert Emmons, a researcher from UC Davis, California, says, "The nature of gratitude has positive consequences for human health and well-being, and that gratitude heals, energizes, and transforms lives." He also suggests that keeping a weekly gratitude journal affects optimism and an interest in helping others.

Gratitude is a form of prayer that helps us develop a new perspective, one that allows us to put on a new pair of glasses. Being thankful fosters an awareness to unfold and the appreciation of the small and large gifts bestowed upon us. This mindset enables us to experience the world differently. Meister Eckhart, a German theologian, philosopher and mystic, says, "If the only prayer you said was thank you, that will suffice."

To truly experience the benefits of gratitude, I began *30 Days of Gratitude*, a daily journal identifying that for which I feel grateful. I offer this list as a prayer to affirm all the blessings I receive. As the days pass, I notice that my shifting perspective can easily show me how abundance manifests and grows within and around me. My journal begins with the words, "Thank you for the ability to walk, talk, see, and hear. And I affirm an appreciation for having the full spectrum of the human experience."

As my gratitude list progresses, I become more and more thankful for my breath and heartbeat as the two vessels that help keep me present in each moment. By the 30th day of journaling, I experience a shift in how I view my life. I feel grateful for the cultivation of my spirit — planted and nurtured as a seedling that cultivates personal growth, creating abundance in the garden of my own life.

Questions to Explore:

1. How do you cultivate gratitude in your daily life?

2. How does gratitude affect you emotionally, physically, cognitively and spiritually?

How Can You Be a Better Parent?

PARENTS ARE PEOPLE GROWERS. Their job is to create an environment where love germinates, flourishes and grows. Our thoughts, emotions and behaviors affect our children, with a cumulative effect on their well-being. We often sleepwalk in our daily lives and are teachers without a formal lesson plan that passes on our values, pain and passions through verbal and non-verbal communications.

Couples choosing to become parents are attracted to each other by both common interests and unresolved childhood pain. It is a match that becomes a conduit to family life and a rite of passage into motherhood and fatherhood. If asked to share my parenting wisdom, I would say begin the journey by envisioning your child as an adult. Attend parenting classes to obtain a lens to view yourself as a parent. Closely monitor your behaviors and emotions, being conscious of the personal pain experienced from your own childhood.

For instance, because I longed for my mother to be more emotionally present, I centered my life around my child. I can clearly see that the unresolved wounds from my past infiltrated my perceptions and limited my ability to be fully mindful of the effects they may have had on my child.

In hindsight, I realize that parenting can create possibilities for personal growth. Although my intentions were rooted in love, the fear that my child would not love me, affected our relationship. If I could have a "redo" and go back in time, I would be more conscious of my own wounds, be less intense, more relaxed, and have had an earlier realization that compensating for what I did not have in my childhood was a mistake.

Jon and Myla Kabat-Zinn in their book, *Everyday Blessings: The Inner Work of Mindful Parenting*, say that "Parenting is one of the most challenging, demanding, and stressful jobs on the planet. It is also one of the most important, for how it is done influences in great measure the heart and soul and consciousness of the next generation, their experience of meaning and connection, their repertoire of life skills, and their deepest feelings about themselves and their possible place in a rapidly changing world."

Parents are the guardians of our children with the responsibility to shift the consciousness of humanity towards compassion and kindness. They are the change agents of society.

Questions to Explore:

1. How has pain from your childhood experiences affected your parenting style?

2. What beliefs about parenting have affected your relationship with your child/children?

How Do Your Relationships
Navigate You Closer
to Your Heart?

RELATIONSHIPS OFTEN PLAY OUT as the drama of human existence. People are both interested in and entertained by the lives of others. Watch any television show or read good fiction, and it becomes apparent that we are social beings programmed to survive by the support of each other. Relationships affect our well-being, and our interactions mirror back what we need to learn about ourselves, giving us feedback to open our hearts to compassion, empathy and wisdom —providing spiritual guidance to help our souls blossom. We learn from our mistakes and those of others. People walk in and out of our lives, as teachers delivering lessons for us to become the author of our own life story. This narrative contributes to the foundation of our spirituality and helps answer that universal question most of us ask, "Who am I?"

Documented in the history of humanity, are many great teachers that share aphorisms as general truths about life. Some of the teachers are Buddha, Ralph Waldo Emerson, and Lao Tzu, each of whom has been credited with the following quote: "Watch your thoughts. They become words. Watch your words. They become deeds. Watch your deeds. They become habits. Watch your habits. They become character. Character becomes your destiny."

Throughout my own inner pilgrimage, I have noticed that relating with others has often been challenging. I have wanted others to give me something that I thought I was not capable of giving to myself, and I was self-critical and unaware of how I projected this negativity. As I become more and more aware of my internal self — my thoughts, emotions, behaviors and bodily sensations — I am able to shift my energy to allow my vibration to be in harmony with the laws of the universe, holding me in the hands of God.

Relationships are made up of a circle of people that reunite with each other. Some we relate to with intimacy, such as family members. Others may be work colleagues, friends, acquaintances, members of spiritual worship or organization, or those who provide services to us. If we are receptive, these interactions can take us on a remarkable journey inward — one that can help us grow into self-awareness. Wayne Dwyer, the late self-help author, and motivational speaker best known for his initial book, *The Erroneous Zones*, said, "How people treat you is their karma; how you react is yours." The way individuals act with me, and how I respond, has helped to create my life story.

Questions to Explore:

1. How do you treat yourself and other people?

2. What relationships have you had that have helped you to grow and made you more self-aware?

Have Life's Loses Fostered
Your Personal Growth?

THERE ARE MANY LOSSES in life. People die. We lose our health. We lose a job. Relationships end. Our beliefs change. We lose our youth. Our identities transform. We may lose personal possessions. How we cope with these losses can affect our mental health. We have the choice to experience loss as part of the metamorphosis of life, to resist grief or remain stuck in incomplete grieving.

Our first loss is leaving the security of our mother's womb. As a baby, when we start to crawl away from our mother, we keep a watchful eye on her, wanting her reassurance. We lose the comfort of our mother's breast. We leave home to go to pre-school and kindergarten. All these events trigger emotions tied to loss. What this shows us is that loss is a part of the shared human experience.

Author and poet Judith Viorst examines the topic of loss in her book, *Necessary Losses*. She says, "The people we are and the lives that we lead are determined, for better and worse, by our loss experiences." We come into the world as dependent beings and develop into being independent adults — a progression of experiences where we lose something we feel is of value, requiring the ability to adjust to the loss.

I take inventory of my own losses. I reminisce over my childhood when I rode my bike, dressed up in my mother's high-heel shoes, and played in my garden. The death of my parents caused a shift within me, giving insight into the temporariness of life. When my son grew up and no longer needed me, I lost my identity as mom.

I remember the day when I saw the changing reflection of my physical body in a mirror and felt its robustness slowly deflate. Then there were the abstract loses, the kind that were not as apparent. Like when my expectations of others were unfulfilled and I felt both angry and sad, or the idea that I could not have what I wanted – and so I believed life was unfair. These are losses that often leave a void that goes unnoticed.

Loss requires a shift in how we perceive the challenges presented. Loss can also offer unexpected opportunities for self-insight, for facilitating an adjustment of beliefs, and for providing the opportunity to grow and evolve as spiritual beings.

Questions to Explore:

1. What losses have you experienced in your life?

2. How did you cope with these losses, and what did you learn from them?

3. How have you evolved as a person through your losses?

What Is It Like to Experience Self-Awareness?

SELF- AWARENESS IS THE state or condition of being conscious of your inner self as you relate to your environment. Developing this awareness begins with the ability to sensitively observe your thoughts, emotions, behaviors, breath and physical sensations. When you develop this skill, everything comes into sharp focus, and then disappears into the background with quiet resolve. It is like performing magic tricks — now you see it, now you feel it, now you experience it, and now it is gone.

Many of us live our lives on autopilot, a state of not being conscious of our inner selves. Instead of truly experiencing a "present" existence, we mostly live in the past or in the future. We develop an unconscious pattern of perceptions from our life experiences that become familiar. Over time, this pattern helps us feel safe and make sense of our world.

Part of personal growth is to develop a spiritual facet of ourselves by paying attention. Emmanuel Swedenborg, a philosopher and theologian whose work is defined as systematic theology, declared that all religions collectively take an honest look at self by acknowledging harmful habits, traits and life patterns. This philosophy helped to contribute to the advancement of religious thought in Christianity and Buddhism, and inspired such great people as Ralph Waldo Emerson and Dr. Carl Jung. At the core of Swedenberg's teachings is the cultivation of consciousness as a religious practice where the soul goes on a daily pilgrimage interweaving the spiritual self with the physical self.

Eckhart Tolle, author of *The Power of Now*, concurs with this philosophy when he states, "Awareness is the greatest agent for change." Daniel Goleman, a modern psychologist and author of "Emotional Intelligence," agrees, "Having the ability to know one's internal states, preferences, resources and intuitions directly affects relationships with self and others which promotes quality of life."

When I lived my life on autopilot as if I were sleep walking, my thoughts about the past and the future determined my mental health. I ignored my "present" and became consumed by the past or worried about the future. I felt afraid, angry and sad. It was by developing self-awareness that helped me awaken to the experience that "the kingdom of God exists within." Luke 17:20-21 (King James Version, 1611). I became aware that cultivating a spiritual life leads to peace.

Having the ability to develop self-awareness comes with the commitment to being present as each moment unfolds. What's more, we have the option to choose different paths to this awakening. It was awareness that became my comfort and helped me to develop empathy and compassion.

Questions to Explore:

1. How do you live your life on autopilot, unaware of your unconscious pattern of perception from your life experiences?

2. What paths of awareness have helped manifest consciousness in your daily life?

What Is the Function of Human Emotions?

E MOTIONS HELP OUR SPECIES survive and care for each other. We were meant to feel our feelings and to give them expression by feeling our emotions and letting them go. Emotions shape the heart, carving space for compassion, love and kindness to thrive. Richard Rohr, a Franciscan priest, says, "Spirituality is invariably a matter of emptying the mind and filling the heart at the same time." Feelings are one of life's teachers catching our attention and helping us awaken to the integrated duality of our physical and spiritual lives.

Emotions are a universal part of the human experience that transform moment to moment. This ebb and flow is the embodiment of being alive. When feelings are ignored or pushed away, they can manifest into negative behaviors, consuming thoughts, or a body that is not in harmony. Many of us have developed our own strategies for handling emotions. Some of us ignore their existence, behave in ways out of the ordinary, suppress, project, or run from our feelings. Others habituate on an addiction of choice that seems to alleviate their pain. The truth is that emotions require both our attention and the courage to embrace whatever feeling is present.

To experience how emotions are part of the human psyche, sit with your feelings as a doorway opening into sacredness.

Ann Frank, who wrote in *The Diary of a Young Girl*, said, "Feelings can't be ignored, no matter how unjust or ungrateful they seem." Betty Smith, author of the book, *A Tree Grows in Brooklyn*, captures the relationship between emotions and our experiences as crucial to understanding life, when she writes, "Dear God, let me be something every minute of every hour of my life. Let me be gay; let me be sad. Let me be cold; let me be warm. Let me be hungry ... have too much to eat. Let me be ragged or well dressed. Let me be sincere — be deceitful. Let me be truthful; let me be a liar. Let me be honorable and let me sin. Only let me be something every blessed minute. And when I sleep, let me dream all the time so that not one little piece of living is ever lost."

Over the years, my emotions have consisted of anger, fear and sadness, sprinkled with moments of joy. I ran from my feelings by being ultra-busy, indulging in unhealthy eating and projecting my behavior onto others. Not allowing myself to feel my emotions caused additional pain. Katie Kacvinsky, an American writer, says, "But pain is like water. It finds a way to push through any seal. There's no way to stop it. Sometimes you have to let yourself sink inside of it, before you can learn how to swim to the surface." Experiencing our emotions is part of being alive. We feel our emotions as an embodied spiritual practice of being human.

Questions to Explore:

1. What emotions have helped to either inhibit or create your life?

2. How do your emotions affect your mental health?

What Does It Mean to be Courageous?

T O BE COURAGEOUS IS to face danger, fear, pain, hardship and uncertainty, without running away. Courage is an act of personal challenge. We read about warriors in mythology and watch movies that portray the expression of the forces of good versus evil. We listen to the news and hear about the sacrifices our soldiers make for our nation's safety and appreciate their valiant acts of courage.

And there is another kind of courage, the kind found in everyday life scenarios that we often do not hear about or even acknowledge as bravery. This valor is in reverence to ordinary people — the heroes and heroines in everyday life. Quiet deeds of courage to be celebrated and recognized as extraordinary and part of the human spirit that offer hope for transformation. These actions can be as simple as facing our deepest fears, taking risks, letting go of negative emotions, staying focused on the present moment despite the obstacles, being adventurous enough to travel down uncharted territory, or allowing ourselves to be vulnerable by expressing our ideas and standing behind our beliefs by our actions.

If we act as if we are brave warriors, we are motivated to face our greatest fears. When we demonstrate courage, we allow ourselves to fail and then get back up and move closer to feeling triumph over our deepest terrors. It is Theodore Roosevelt who said, "It is not the critic who counts; not the man who points out how the strong man stumbles, or where the doer of deeds could have done them better. The credit belongs to the man who is actually in the arena, whose face is marred by dust and sweat and blood; who strives valiantly; who errs, who comes short again and again, because there is no effort without error and shortcoming; but who does actually strive to do the deeds; who knows great enthusiasms, the great devotions; who spends himself in a worthy cause; who at the best knows in the end the triumph of high achievement, and who at the worst, if he fails, at least fails while daring greatly, so that his place shall never be with those cold and timid souls who neither know victory nor defeat."

Having courage is part of the expression of the soul. It is what Joseph Campbell, known for his work in comparative mythology and religion, calls "The Hero's Journey." A male/female archetype goes on a mystical pilgrimage to achieve a great deed on behalf of their group, tribe, or civilization. This universal calling requires inner strength, courage, and the motivation to meet these challenges. Sustaining these trials requires bravery and the desire to return home to the place of the heart that holds the ultimate expression of Divine love.

There are many times that I have fallen and then was able to regain my balance. This strength began when I became more conscious of my inheritance, the intergenerational connection of the women in my family who did not feel loved or nurtured. So my spiritual evolution required that I become attentive to finding self-love. As a person with a learning disability, I worked harder than my peers and had to accept those times when I felt that I was good enough. Having health challenges that were accompanied by the diagnosis of Lyme's Disease requires the courage to accept what life hands me – and bravely focus on my own healing path. Both my learning disability and health challenges were life teachers helping me to learn to love myself.

Questions to Explore:

1. How have you been a hero or heroine in your own life?

2. What quiet deeds of courage have helped to transform you?

What Can Your Dog Teach You?

THE GREATEST STORIES EVER told come from the heart, accounting for the loving energy that joins living beings to each other and to a force greater than ourselves.

Grace was a black and white Shih Tzu who we jokingly called our "designer dog." She had one blue eye and one brown eye and always took pride in wearing her colorful bows. She was also our "uptown dog" because she preferred sidewalks and shopping, to grass and the park. Gracie, as we called her, loved people and never turned down a cookie. The story of her life was one of unconditional love accompanied by deep affection and friendship — the kind that many of us ache to experience.

I remember the day we drove to a farm in the country with our black and white Shih Tzu named Calvin, in search of a dog companion for him. I have a flashback of Calvin peering through the door of the farmhouse which opened onto a porch where all the puppies were playing. He sat on the other side of the glass watching his human parents talk to the owner of the farm. All of a sudden, we looked and there were two dogs sitting there watching us! Little eight-week old Gracie sat next to her soon-to-be brother Calvin and watched with curiosity to see what he was looking at. This memory is how our bond began and became the story of the day Grace picked her family and how we fell in love.

The word "Grace" is defined as the bestowal of blessings. As fate revealed, she became a real blessing and one of my greatest teachers. She taught me many things my soul needed to know about the real gifts of life:

- She stayed in the present moment with no thoughts of her past or concern for the future. Instead, she remained in a peaceful state of consciousness.
- When she walked to the park and other dogs annoyed her, she would take care of herself by turning and walking home as if she thought, "I've had enough of this."
- If she was tired, she would listen to her little body and take a nap. She would awaken refreshed and ready to begin again.
- When her physical health started to change, she was able to make adjustments and still find ways to enjoy her life.
- If she fell down, she would get right back up and continue walking.
- Whatever challenges that life presented, she kept moving with the confidence that all would be OK.
- She always took time to smell the grass, feel the breeze, and experience her daily life with zest and wonder.

Gracie Ann passed on July 7, 2015, into the loving hands of our creator. She will always hold a loving memory in my heart. Her presence will be eternally alive within me always — held by the love we had for each other.

Questions to Explore:

1. How are you able to stay in a peaceful state of consciousness?

2. What do you feel are the real gifts of life?

How Does Trauma Affect You?

TRAUMA IS SOMETHING MOST of us experience in our lives. The Merriam-Webster dictionary defines trauma as "a very difficult or unpleasant experience that often causes someone to have mental or emotional problems over a long period." Mark Goulston, in his book, *Post-Traumatic Stress Disorder for Dummies*, writes, "Unlike simple stress, trauma changes your view of your life and yourself. It shatters your most basic assumptions and your world — life is good, I am safe and people are kind — to be replaced with feelings like the world is dangerous, I can't win or trust others and there is no hope."

Lisa Wimberger, author of *Neurosculpting*, says, "The limbic system of the brain is programmed for survival, and has become so efficient that it easily forgets the difference between a real threat and a perceived threat. When the brain remembers a strong story from the past, the body believes it is real and fires up the nervous system." If we are not taught how our brain operates and how to develop the skills to cope with trauma in our lives, the triggering of the fight/flight mechanism for survival will initiate flashbacks, nightmares, stress symptoms, the perseverance of negative thoughts, and an overflowing of emotions that seeps into our hearts, becoming the barrier to experiencing peace.

The nightly news on television appears to validate an increase in violence, crime, abuse, poverty, homelessness, and natural disasters affecting all of us. These stories are a reflection of the condition of humankind. Anna Funder in her novel, *All That I Am*, writes, "Most people have no imagination. If they could imagine the suffering of others, they would not make them suffer so." As a society, we are often unaware of the depth of anguish that humans experience. How we treat each other becomes our history. On a personal level, this translates into how individuals may feel and think – and the way they store the traumatic memories their bodies holds cellularly.

Marilyn Van Derbur, in her book, *Miss America by Day: Lessons Learned from Ultimate Betrayals and Unconditional Love*, says, "All emotions, even those that are suppressed and unexpressed, have physical effects. Unexpressed emotions tend to stay in the body like small ticking time bombs — they are illnesses in incubation." As a society, this manifests into how we nurture and raise our children and how we treat each other. It also helps explain the way groups are formulated and shaped by our culture.

From a larger perspective, the systems we develop to organize and cope with our failings, promotes suffering. For example, the prisons we build to address the consequences of crime or the elaborate mental and physical health systems intended to heal, are both part of our collective consciousness created to help, but they, instead, often cause additional pain. Trauma is born from the ways we consciously or unconsciously treat each other.

I am a veteran of this same ribbon of trauma that has played itself out in my own life, as it has for many. I create narratives that link me to the same-themed stories that involve unstable attachments. As a willing victim of others' unconscious behaviors, I formulated a residue of unexpressed fear, anger and grief. This is descriptive of the world where we all live, play and weep when an individual or institution experiences suffering.

Questions to Explore:

1. What traumatic experiences have you had in your life?

2. How has trauma affected your health, relationships, emotions and thinking?

What Has Suffering Taught You?

S UFFERING IS THE STATE of undergoing pain, distress, or hardship. The anguish of suffering is programmed into the human experience, eliciting emotions that are an integral part of our soul's journey. Often, we call upon our higher power for solace during times of suffering. Major religions of the world all speak of suffering as being an integral part of becoming enlightened. Judaism, Christianity, Buddhism, Islam and Hinduism all agree that pain is a catalyst for deepening our spirit. Author and psychiatrist, the late Elizabeth Kubler Ross, who wrote about the stages of grief, speaks about stepping into suffering as being courageous and transformative when she says, "Should you shield canyons from wind storms you would never see the true beauty of their carvings."

In her book, *Tears to Triumph*, author and spiritual teacher, Marianne Williamson talks about our spiritual journey as being on a continuum – from suffering to enlightenment. She says, "The pain you are going through is not what will determine your future; your future will be determined by who you are as you go through pain." This pilgrimage is a spiritual passage where we learn from our actions and interactions with others, helping us to become spiritually literate.

A friend of mine asked, "What has suffering taught you?" This question helped me to realize that to be human means that you inevitably experience what it means to hurt. Human beings connect with each other through suffering. It is how we develop empathy, compassion and kindness. There are some of us who are more wounded than others. However, if we are receptive to growing into our highest self, we can develop an inner depth, strength and awareness. Khalil Gibran, a Lebanese American poet, says, "Out of suffering have emerged the strongest souls; the most massive characters are seared scars."

Having a spiritual path means following a direction that guides us towards our true purpose. For me, not feeling loved has been a wound that has created suffering in my life. My purpose is to learn how to love myself. As an adult, my job is to expand the feelings of joy, peace and love that I so desperately want to experience. Kahlil Gibran speaks my truth (and maybe that of others) when he articulates, "And God said, "Love your enemy," and I obeyed him, and loved myself."

Self-love is the foundation for our mental/emotional and physical health, as well as the quality of our relationships. It is an antidote to suffering, for when we love ourselves we nourish our own growth and development, leaving space for the thriving of our heart's desire.

Questions to Explore:

1. How has suffering affected your life?

2. What has suffering taught you?

How Can Faith Be Integrated into Daily Life?

FAITH IS THE WILLINGNESS to believe without proof that something you know is true. This belief comes from deep within, yet there are many of us who struggle with how to experience something that is not seen, heard or logical. "Now faith is the substance of things hoped for, the evidence of things not seen." Hebrews 11:1 (King James Version, 1611). For me, the desire to stand grounded in my ability to live with faith has grown as I have gained life experience.

It is free will that allows us to decide whether to defer to faith or live in fear. The poet and philosopher from the nineteenth century, Rabindranath Tagore, said, "Faith is the light when the dawn is still dark." During times when darkness falls, recognize that life is in perpetual motion and everything changes. Knowing this gives us hope that there are two sides to our emotional experiences. There are those emotions that we want to avoid, and those we want to embrace.

Some of us are experts at avoiding feeling sad, angry or afraid. This often translates into addictions or other types of behaviors that can easily affect relationships. Most people want to live in the light of sunshine, bathing in joy, love and peace. Both challenging and positive feelings are in juxtaposition to one another, creating a full spectrum of emotions. And like the two sides of the Chinese symbol yin and yang, we aspire to maintain dynamic balance between the two.

As an experiment, I am contemplating the idea of letting go and dancing with a companion instead of going solo. This requires exploring new ways of how to sense, feel and be in harmony with a partner who will harmonize with me towards expanding my soul. Learning how to tango with conviction is a metaphor for my relationship with God, and an avenue for exploring what it means to have faith. This dance entails developing the ability to know when to lead or follow, when to stay close or leave space, or when to pause — all while letting go and trusting that my partner holds me with open arms.

Developing the skill needed to tango is my way of developing faith. I am motivated to show up and dance, practice daily, and experience the sensation of how these new movements can imprint as my heart's desire. My new partner is my higher self, directing me to live with trust. Saint Augustine, an early Christian theologian and philosopher, said, "Pray as though everything depends on God. Work as though everything depends on you." And so, I do both – pray to God and work on my enlightenment, knowing that this relationship is based on personal choice and the desire to live in peace.

Most of us want to believe that there is something that is far greater than ourselves. That we are all beneficiaries of love, offering meaning to our lives. The dance of life is our teacher sent to help us develop faith in ourselves and each other. Faith opens the doors and windows to our spirit and is the gift of hope that makes the experience of living worthwhile.

Questions to Explore:

1. Has life itself been a teacher that has helped you to develop faith?

2. Do you have faith in something larger than yourself? If so, how has this affected your life and spiritual growth?

What Are You Thinking?

Y OU MUST CHANGE YOUR negative thoughts if you want to transform your life. John Kehoe, author of *Mind Power Basics*, says, "Your thoughts are vibrations of energy that have a powerful influence; they affect what happens to you." Thoughts create your experiences. Becoming mindful of this universal truth begins with self-exploration and the ability to take inventory of your whole-body intelligence.

Taisen Deshimaru, founder of the Association of Zen International, says, "Think with the whole body." In other words, become aware of your thoughts, emotions, body movements and sensations because they develop into patterns and life perceptions. Many of us may be oblivious to or ignore this fundamental process of becoming conscious of how to communicate with our deepest self. To quote Marianne Williamson again, "You are responsible for what you think, because it is only at this level that you can exercise choice. What you do comes from what you think."

I select my thoughts just like the daily clothes I choose to wear. Some thoughts are rooted in my core belief about self. Others are caring and thoughtful. Then there are thoughts that are practical, the kind that orchestrate the tasks of daily living.

I hold thoughts linked to my history as if they were sewn together like pieces of a quilt, visually capturing past wounds. I practice the act of emptying my mind of all thoughts during meditation. I notice that my thoughts become verbs as I plan, ruminate, and transform into the focused energy of a conductor playing a unique symphony.

As I reflect on my own thought process, I am reminded of a teenage girl I once helped. She was incapacitated by thoughts that held her head hostage, aching with no joy or peace. Some may say she was clinically depressed. Her peer relationships were a source of emotional pain. She filtered her world by what she thought she saw, heard or believed to be true. This distorted thinking made suicide permissible, and its consequence was left for her intimate circle to endure.

In our culture, we often experience being judged, criticized, inadequate and rejected. This universal theme keeps us in a web of negative thinking, holding us in a pattern of feeling as if we are "not enough." This very thinking evolves into good versus bad judgments, rather than the acceptance of what is. And like habits that we develop, we store these in our brain and body as suffering, with no formal training on how to deal with our heartache.

What we say to ourselves allows us to interpret our experiences from our own perspective. If we view our thoughts as if we are watching a movie, we become observers. Becoming a "Life Watcher" helps us become responsible for our thinking. This awareness allows us to make choices; we can choose to become lost in thought, stuck on words, or we can access our self-talk like a sage, navigating through the terrain of our lives. This dialogue becomes the wise part of self, and an inner voice programmed to listen.

Questions to Explore:

1. If you were to divide your daily thoughts into a pie chart, what possibilities could this create for your life?

2. Do you have core belief about self, and how does this affect your thinking?

How Might You Live Each
Day Like It Is Your Last?

DYING IS PART OF the process of living. We are born to
die. From the moment we enter the physical realm,
we are preparing and practicing for the transformation that
occurs when our body stops functioning. The purpose of our
physical life is for the soul to grow and expand, change, and
evolve our spirituality. It is this evolution — based on the
act of letting go — that allows the self to be born and reborn
again and again.

Immediately upon birth, the journey towards death
begins. Death is the great equalizer, and whether a person
is rich or poor, holds notoriety or ordinary status, the end is
inevitable. Steve Jobs, the founder of Apple Computers, once
said, "No one wants to die. Even people who want to go to
heaven don't want to die to get there. And yet death is the
destination we all share. No one has ever escaped it. Death is
very likely the single best invention of life. It is life's change
agent. It clears out the old to make way for the new."

I am an intermittent yogini, the female version of a yogi,
who has returned to yoga after a period of abstinence. In
class, my body becomes relaxed, mindful, and focused. At its

conclusion, I lie in the corpse pose to practice the act of letting go in preparation for my death. As a student who engages in stillness, I understand that this pose requires practice.

Whatever we aspire to be, whether it is a writer, artist or scholar, it requires frequent rehearsal. When we observe life, we see the daily unfolding of birth and death. This process is found in nature, the animal kingdom, and in the development of our own spirituality. We die and are reborn to create new visions and ways of being in the world.

Western philosophers offer advice to prepare us for the inevitable, telling us to live each day as if it were our last. This means watching life unfold, doing what you love, and being kinder and gentler to ourselves and others. Tim McGraw, a Country Western singer, summarized this sentiment in the song, *Live Like You Were Dying*. After being faced with the possibility of physical death, he sings, "I went sky diving, and Rocky Mountain climbing, loved deeper, spoke sweeter, and gave forgiveness, all for the chance to live like I was dying."

This message makes me reflect on my college days when I was given a class assignment to write my own eulogy. The instructions were to envision how others would remember me at my funeral. This process helped me realize that I am no different than my peers. I discovered that most of my classmates were not interested in being remembered for their accomplishments or possessions, but rather for those memories that reflect the presence of the heart, those connections that are expressions of love.

Questions to Explore:

1. What might contemplating death teach you about living?

2. What if today is your last day, what would you do differently?

What Is Your Intention?

A N INTENTION IS A powerful form of energy that, when accompanied by clarity, determination and focus, becomes a prevailing entity. James Redfield, author of the inspirational fiction, *The Celestine Prophecy*, says, "The basic stuff of the universe, at its core, is looking like a kind of pure energy that is malleable to human intention and expectation." I believe intentionality is developed through the power of devotion, an ongoing prayer that transcends the soul.

One of my intentions during childhood was to learn how to play the violin. I could visualize watching the bow move and then become still. When I touched the violin, my hands followed its curves, plucked it cords, and felt the smooth, glossy wooden finish. I listened to its sounds, sensed its vibrations, and felt its profound resonance within my soul. The strings pulled me inward where my intuitive self knew that making music holds space for loving kindness to thrive.

With introspection, I understand that I create my life by asking, "What is my intention?" I respond to this question by recognizing two components of my deepest desire. My first intention belongs to the symbol of a heart – I intend to see, feel, and sense love in all aspects of life. My second intention is the symbol of an owl, the power animal that is a spirit guide sent to help me develop wisdom. I intend to bring my attention to experiences occurring in the present moment that encompass my inner self and my external environment. Together, the heart and the owl represent self-knowledge and wisdom, that which is most important to my spiritual growth. Intention becomes the seedling for a new creation, and in a tangible form, becomes the inner guidance that gives birth to an expanded form of consciousness. This insight allows me to go beyond my ego and into the realm of silence that becomes a form of meditation. Being aware of these two desires helps me to trust in a power that can create infinite possibilities.

I have developed my own path to intention similar to the way an artist magically makes something out of nothing. These six steps mystically unfolded into the list identified below. They are instructions presented in a linear sequence, which I believe needs to be fine-tuned by each person, so some of the steps may overlap, some may occur together, or others may be totally omitted. You decide by allowing your awareness and your heart to be your guide.

- Choose an intention that represents the greatest good.
- Develop clarity about what you want to manifest by using positive language.
- Visualize a picture (mine is a heart and an owl) that you can watch in your mind's eye and breathe into throughout the day.
- Believe your intention is a gift to yourself and others.
- Thank God for its manifestation in your life.
- Watch how the creation process reveals itself

Questions to Explore:

1. What is your intention for your life?

2. How can you turn an intention into a prayer?

What Makes You Sad?

OWN AN OLD, WORN duffle bag that is stuffed with sadness. It sits in the corner of my bedroom floor as unobtrusive clutter. I try to ignore this sadness but my tears fall. Paul Coelho, the author of *The Alchemist*, says, "Tears are words that need to be written." So here I sit, writing about the accumulation of sadness that waits to be set free. My words become sentences that connect sorrow from past to the present. These are my sacred conversations with self and a holy reflection that transforms the soul. My most pressing story is held in my heart, and rooted from childhood — not feeling loved.

Most of us have acquired reasons to feel sad. So I acknowledge this list of perceptions as seeing them as branches of a tree that connect to its trunk. The pain is cumulative and reflects history documented by the years that I have lived. My mother left me feeling sad. My son exited from the family we once were. My dog passed on, leaving a void. There is an ongoing struggle to regain the vibrant health I once had. I am aging, and the person I once was does not look the same. There are those relationships that never gave birth to love and a part of me that is not able to be consoled.

Thinking about the children who don't have adequate parenting, I see my own self-image in a mirror. I realize that some of those children will grow up sooner, some later, and still others never do. Yet, many remain the older version of a child that still cries. I have been one of those children who grew up and worked hard to allow my soul to evolve. My formula for personal growth naturally evolved. It begins with prayer and meditation to clear my thoughts. I focus my intention on love and self-awareness. I feed my soul through writing. I pay attention to what my body communicates. And lastly, I am willing to acknowledge those parts of me that are ashamed, yet willing to be courageous enough to continue to grow spiritually.

Clive Barker, author of the fantasy novel, *Days of Magic, Nights of War,* says, "Any fool can be happy. It takes a man with real heart to make beauty out of the stuff that makes us weep." As I matured, I realized that sadness offers its own pearls of wisdom. Sadness can become a compassion-builder that develops empathy and insight to bridge a connection to the highest good. It can be a teacher that helps modify behavior in a kinder and gentler way to help judgments dissipate, for we all travel down similar paths.

Ultimately, there is the realization that we are social beings that need each other to prosper. When we can stand together and acknowledge our tears, our pain can be eased — leading us down the mystical path where love, peace and joy flourish.

Questions to Explore:

1. What makes you sad?

2. How has your sadness taught you anything about what it is like to experience humanness?

How Are You Able to
Recognize Your Own Fear?

F EAR IS THE REACTION to the awareness of potential
harm. It is an instinctual response called the fight/
flight mechanism that senses danger when personal safety
is threatened. This physiological response is innate and
programmed for survival. Fear activates our entire organism,
moving us away from danger to ensure the preservation of the
species. Our body self-regulates with continuity and fluidity,
vacillating between the sympathetic and the parasympathetic
nervous system, becoming concise movements that define
daily life as capturing spirituality unfolding from vigilance
to calmness and back again.

Being scared, clinically, is a human emotion that can
be defined as trauma, with a potential for self-sabotage
and destruction. This emotion left unchecked can become
a barrier for experiencing our true self. Chronic fear can
sacrifice our life, not during the times when there is imminent
danger, but rather when our thoughts become challenging
emotions, frozen in space. This is when we relive what
makes us afraid by what we think, bodily sensations, and
challenging emotions that repeat themselves. When fear

becomes a repetitive cycle, it can create our life story, often at the expense of self and others.

In 1872, Charles Darwin, an English naturalist, wrote a scientific evolutionary theory and the book, *The Expressions of the Emotions in Man and Animals*. He suggests that emotions are vitality in motion; that is, energy that sustains human survival. When emotions are stagnant, the intent is to feel safe.

Our behaviors are often created to survive and are accompanied by the avoidance of what feels most painful. Aeschylus, an ancient Greek tragedian known as the father of tragedy said, "There are times when fear is good. It must keep its watchful place at the heart's control." These words of wisdom can motivate all of us to perfect our skills, try harder, love more, and be the bearer of random acts of kindness, knowing that the courageous heart can set us free.

Kay Redfield Jamison, an American clinical psychologist, said, "There is always a part of my mind that is preparing for the worst, and another part of my mind that believes if I prepare enough for it, the worst won't happen." This concisely describes the predicament of trauma – the preservation of self as avoidance of fear versus losing out on the gifts of facing our fears.

My perceptions about life were often accompanied by the fear of rejection that followed obsessive thinking and behaviors rooted by the need to protect myself from feeling afraid. Somewhere along the journey, I identified the avenues that made me feel emotionally safe. These strategies evolved as overeating, overthinking, and avoiding emotions and relationships.

What we see, think, and feel often is how a life story is written and repeated. For me, the sensate component of fear accompanies anxiety and is caused by reoccurring anger that promotes isolation and separation from God. Yet, my heart's desire is to stop responding to fear and to let go, becoming more intimate with the feeling of joy. This yearning became the path to my spiritual growth. I could either choose universal oneness, or be separated from love. I choose love.

Questions to Explore:

1. How is being afraid shaped your thoughts, emotions and relationships?

2. How might fear motivate you to be your best self?

What Is Your Experience
with Money?

JOSE ORTEGA Y GASSET was a Spanish philosopher who wrote, "In beliefs we live, we move and we are, and that belief constitute the base of our life."

Many of our beliefs about money originate from our families, those first-hand experiences that become the stories that arise out of our minds and shape our reality about abundance. We do not have enough, we have too much, or we are afraid of losing what we have. My parents owned their own business and were forced into bankruptcy. We lost our home, and as a teenager, I had to work to pay for my own clothes, while watching my friends easily receive what they wanted or needed. As a result, I held anxiety about not having enough money or losing what I had. My narrative was based on the fear of being homeless, and I felt resentment as I watched others go on vacations or buy the clothes they wanted. I used money to show myself love by buying things, and then regretted being irresponsible about my spending. Having nice things validated my worth.

This unconscious relationship between myself and money became the conditioned feeling of constraint. I ranged from feeling imprisoned to enlightened by the transformative power that grows with self-awareness. I had a problem with money because of the beliefs and conflicts that existed in my own mind. I focused on not having enough, and I had limited appreciation of the resources I held within my heart, or in my home where I had a closet filled with clothes. It was my ability to become more aware of my beliefs about money that eventually broke my trance and helped me understand that abundance is always available and that the universe holds enough for all of us.

Money elicits both emotional responses and logic from humans. It has its own language, one that the ego and the soul understand. They are partners in communication, speaking to each other through the beliefs and the cells of our bodies. Their message determines and creates how and when abundance flows or remains stagnant. This energy becomes the tide of our own perceptions that can vacillate between wealth and deprivation. We decide whether to save, spend, generate more, or give in the spirit of generosity. Some say that the more you give, the more you will receive. Regardless, we all have a choice in how we view our personal resources. We can worry about not having enough, being fearful by holding on to what we have, or trusting that we will receive what we need. It is almost as if a spell holds many of us hostage to our uncertainties, a habitual motion between self-worth and essence.

Dr. Bruce Lipton, PhD, is a cell biologist and pioneer in new biology and author of *The Biology of Belief*, who says that all the cells in our body are affected by our thoughts, which are generated by our beliefs about our lives. The late Candace Pert, PhD, and neuroscientist known for the book,

Molecules of Emotions, also supported the idea that the body and mind function as part of an interconnected system where chemicals effect our beliefs, emotions, health and how we create our lives. Jose Ortega y Gasset says, "Tell me what you pay attention to and I will tell you who you are." So, if you focus your fears on money, it will affect every aspect of your life.

Our experiences help us develop beliefs about how we spend, save and manage money. Money is a metaphor for an energy exchange that effects our lives, involving the interactions of our thoughts, emotions and body, all components of our human and spiritual development.

Questions to Explore:

1. What are your beliefs about money?

2. How have these beliefs affected how you handle and manage abundance?

What Does Your Heart Know?

THE HEART KNOWS. IT has its own language. In the book entitled *A Course of Love*, the author and First Receiver, Mari Perron tells us, "The law of spiritual freedom is the freedom that lies beyond belief, beyond thought, beyond adherence to any authority other than its own heart." When the heart is wounded, it becomes closed, afraid and angry. This is often accompanied by heartless actions and heartache. When the heart is open, it is free and often accompanied by joy and a sense of peace. The heart has its own intelligence, and emotions that communicate through both love and the physical expression of the body's central nervous system.

The Heart Math Institute is a non-profit company established in 1991 to support the idea that the heart plays an integral role in formulating patterns that modify brain function and affect our perceptions, cognition, emotional states and ability to function. The company's mission is "to help people bring their physical, mental, and emotional systems into balanced alignment with their intuitive guidance."

The heart represents the symbol for love, for without love, human beings would not exist. Love embraces our higher self, that which nourishes the soul. The heart creates a person's life story. We have the free will to choose between our thoughts and beliefs and whether we establish a connection to God. To experience life through the presence of the heart is powerful. The heart provides a spiritual choice – to live in love or to live in fear. This truth is illustrated by a person's perceptions and response to the world.

To this point, I want to share an observation. This universal story is written in parables found in holy religious books and in mythology. It reflects the hero/heroine's journey to choose between good versus evil, mirroring the trials of the heart. For all of us, our journey begins with simple everyday choices in life that cause the heart to open or close. We evolve from birth to death and rebirth, with the potential outcome of spiritual transformation. Each of us gets to choose to either create a closed heart or an open heart. The closed heart is filled with fear. It is broken into tiny little pieces that are naked, exposed and vulnerable. The open heart floats freely and lightly, part of the spiritual quest.

At this time, I invite you to explore your own heart. To reflect back to that initial wound captured in your life. Visualize how the colors, textures, shapes and figures became its own art. Ask yourself what the crucial relationships were, or the moments in time, that were sequestered into the cells of your body, the pulse of your heart and the frozen thought process of your brain? However you react to that image, know the truth is that the heart feels, the heart creates, and the heart experiences its own perception that provides a compass to your inner self.

Questions to Explore:

1. What is the status of your heart – is it opened, closed or does it sometimes change?

2. What has been that one-snapshot of your heart that captures your life as an image?

What Are You Willing to Accept?

A CCEPTANCE IS THE ACT of being tolerant of something or someone, which can be an expression of sacredness – a universal theme woven into the religions of the world. This viewpoint is born out of the womb of inner silence, accompanied by faith and an unfolding sense of peace. We live our lives by how we think, feel and behave, creating the ability to enjoy life that can manifest as happiness. The actor Michael J. Fox, said, "My happiness grows in direct proportion to my acceptance, and in inverse proportion to my expectations."

The dominant culture holds values and beliefs that originate in our inner voice. It is programmed to tell you what is wrong with you in contrast to what is right about you. We create these stories by believing what we tell ourselves — often focusing on our frailties instead of our gifts. The context of each of our lives may be different, but our energetic patterns are consistently released into the universe. They are accompanied by messengers, those triggers (which are people, places, events or things) sent to help release internalized past emotions that remain frozen by time. I am no different than my readers. My inner voice and perceptions about the world are to a considerable extent programmed to judge, criticize and focus on inadequacies. This was especially so as a younger person. I was blinded by this negativity and found it difficult to feel and see through my heart. My inner dialogue was not nurturing or tolerant of myself or others. Instead of accepting, suffering became my resistance to perceived unfairness, along with the desire to control the outcomes of my own experiences.

Life provides many opportunities for acceptance which can be part of a spiritual practice. There are four steps that spirituality/religion may define as primary prevention to what is defined as mental health:

1. Pray, ask the divine to help you see your goodness and to love and accept yourself and others as they are. Another way of saying this is to put on a new pair of glasses to see the world from a different perspective.

2. Take inventory of your daily blessings. For example, this can be as simple as being either a donor or recipient of random acts of kindness.

3. Problem-solve situations as they present themselves. For example, I purchased clothing and discovered I was charged two times for the same merchandise. Initially, when I realized that this occurred, I felt angry, which motivated me to remediate the situation.

4. Exhale — breathe in and out to the count of four, and let go. Stop trying to control the outcomes of your life. Cultivate the ability to welcome whatever presents opportunities for self-insight and character development.

Tara Brach, an American psychologist who specializes in Buddhist teaching for emotional healing, says, "The only way to live is by accepting each minute as an unrepeatable miracle." She further states, "Recognizing what is happening inside, and regarding what we see with an open, kind and loving heart, is called "Radical Acceptance." If we are holding back from any part of our experience, if our heart shuts out any part of who we are and what we feel, we are fueling the fears and feelings of separation that sustain the trance of unworthiness." I believe that in God's eyes we are all worthy.

I ask myself, "What am I willing to accept?" Then I think of the *Serenity Prayer* written in 1951 by the American Theologian, Reinhold Niebuhr. These words have become the sentiments that comfort me. "God, grant me the serenity to accept the things I cannot change. The courage to change the things I can, and wisdom to know the difference."

Questions to Explore:

1. What are the opportunities for acceptance in your life to be part of a daily spiritual practice?

2. What are you willing to accept for your life?

Epilogue

Will the Questions Cease?

N OW THAT YOU HAVE joined me on my journey and started your own path to awareness, I invite you to continue to be a "Life Watcher," asking questions and looking for the answers from your inner self. I have always been curious about life and motivated to ask questions. The desire to recognize something far greater than self turned into part of my daily ritual. My quest to understand became an avenue to experiencing my true essence. The path towards consciousness became the embodiment of devotion by transforming self-loathing into self-love.

Questioning led to personal growth which accompanied self-insight into the part of myself that I denied. It is what the late psychiatrist Carl Jung defines as the "shadow side of self," the part of the ego that suppresses consciousness until light shines on the unknown part of self. As part of the process of delving inward, I discovered that not feeling nurtured created my life story.

As I became more aware of my thoughts and emotions, I discovered that the pilgrimage into my inner self helped me to be aware of the sediments of anger, fear and grief that occurred over many years. This became the basis for understanding how everything begins and ends with self.